Finally, the concluding section makes a
thorough survey of all the existing criticism
written in England, America, and France,
with particular attention to Miss Compton-
Burnett's relation to the French novelist and
critic, Nathalie Sarraute. Attention is also
given, in a separate section, to those critics
who have presented the most trenchant adverse assessments of Miss Compton-Burnett's
novels.

The work was carried out with the generous help of the author herself, who cor-
responded extensively with Mr. Baldanza
while he was working on this study. She was
especially helpful in answering questions that
arose in relation to the novels and to her
general ideas about writing.

ABOUT THE AUTHOR ...

Dr. Frank Baldanza is an alumnus of
Oberlin College (1949), with graduate degrees from The University of Chicago (1950)
and Cornell University (1954). He has
taught English at The Georgia Institute of
Technology, Louisiana State University, and
Bowling Green State University. His writ-
ings include *Mark Twain: An Introduction
and Interpretation* in addition to articles in
*American Literature, Modern Fiction Stud-
ies,* and other scholarly and critical journals.
He is a member of Phi Beta Kappa and The
Modern Language Association of America.

Twayne's English Authors Series

Sylvia E. Bowman, *Editor*

INDIANA UNIVERSITY

Ivy Compton-Burnett

Ivy Compton-Burnett

By FRANK BALDANZA

Bowling Green State University

Twayne Publishers, Inc. :: New York

For: *My Parents*

Preface

Ivy Compton-Burnett is neither widely known nor widely read by the general public; on the other hand, literary specialists and fellow writers who know her work are almost uniformly enthusiastic about both the profundity of moral insight and the highly literate wit that characterize her work. The purpose of this volume is to survey and assess the quality of her achievement for the general reader so that the enduring value of her work may reach a wider public.

The first chapter presents the available biographical material, followed by a longer analysis of the general content of the novels; it concludes with a preliminary treatment of Miss Compton-Burnett's technique and the literary values of her work. Chapters 2 through 4 consist of a chronological survey of the nineteen novels. The final chapter surveys English, American, and French criticism of the novels.

As W. H. Auden recently pointed out, book reviewing should be devoted entirely to telling potential readers whether they would like this or that new work; criticism, ideally, should be addressed to those readers who are already acquainted with a literary work and who wish to compare their impressions with those of another reader. In terms of this distinction, I have tried to strike a balance between review and criticism in the hope that this book will introduce new readers to Miss Compton-Burnett's work and at the same time provide the seasoned Compton-Burnett reader with a balanced criticism of her high achievement.

I wish to record my gratitude to the late Mrs. Norbert F. O'Donnell for her kind help in reading the manuscript and to Drs. Morris and Hilda Golden and Mr. Francis W. Schork for their discussions of the work and their encouragement. My deepest debt is to Miss Compton-Burnett herself, who kindly and unfailingly responded to all my questions.

FRANK BALDANZA

Bowling Green State University
May, 1964

Acknowledgments

Curtis Brown, Ltd., and Harcourt, Brace & World, Inc., for permission to quote from *Men and Wives* and *A Family and a Fortune.*

Farrar, Straus and Cudahy, Inc., for permission to quote from *The Contemporary English Novel* by Frederick Robert Karl.

Ivor Nicholson and Watson, Ltd., for permission to quote from *Orion.*

Harper & Row, Publishers, for permission to quote from Arnold Kettle's *An Introduction to the English Novel.*

Simon and Schuster, Inc., for permission to quote from *The Mighty and Their Fall* and *A Heritage and Its History.*

Julian Messner, Inc., for permission to quote from *Mother and Son* and *A Father and His Fate* (for U. S. only).

Martin Secker and Warburg, Ltd., for permission to quote from Edward Sackville-West, *Inclinations.*

Alfred A. Knopf, Inc., for permission to quote from *Darkness and Day, Two Worlds and Their Ways,* and *Bullivant and the Lambs.*

Jonathan Cape, Ltd., for permission to quote from Robert Liddell's *A Treatise on the Novel.*

Peter Owen, Ltd., for permission to quote from Kenneth Alsop's *The Angry Decade.*

Victor Gollancz for permission to quote from *Parents and Children, Pastors and Masters,* and *Elders and Betters.*

George Braziller, Inc., for permission to quote from *The Age of Suspicion* by Nathalie Sarraute.

Contents

Chronology

1892 Ivy Compton-Burnett was born in London.
1902 Entered Royal Holloway College, London University.
1903 Passed Intermediate Arts Examination.
1904 Awarded Founder's Scholarship.
1906 Passed Bachelor of Arts Honors Examination (Classics, Class II).
1907 Left Royal Holloway College.
1911 *Dolores* (dates of the novels are those of the British publication).
1925 *Pastors and Masters.*
1929 *Brothers and Sisters.*
1931 *Men and Wives.*
1933 *More Women than Men.*
1935 *A House and Its Head.*
1937 *Daughters and Sons.*
1939 *A Family and a Fortune.*
1941 *Parents and Children.*
1944 *Elders and Betters.*
1947 *Manservant and Maidservant.* Published in the United States in 1948 as *Bullivant and the Lambs.*
1949 *Two Worlds and Their Ways.*
1951 *Darkness and Day.* Miss Compton-Burnett was made a Commander of the Order of the British Empire in the birthday honors.
1953 *The Present and the Past.*
1955 *Mother and Son.*
1956 Awarded the James Tait Black Memorial Prize.
1957 *A Father and His Fate.*
1959 *A Heritage and Its History.*
1960 Received Doctor of Letters degree, University of Leeds.
1961 *The Mighty and Their Fall.*
1963 *A God and His Gifts.*

Ivy Compton-Burnett

CHAPTER 1

My Own Way

> "I cannot tell you why I write as I do, as I
> do not know. I have even tried not to do it,
> but find myself falling back into my own
> way."—Ivy Compton-Burnett

I *Biography*

AFTER a halting start, Miss Ivy Compton-Burnett has produced a novel of extraordinarily high quality every other
year on the odd year since 1929, with only two interruptions—
during World War II. The force of discipline implied by such
production is one of the primary components of an art that is
distinctive for its austerity, intelligence, economy, and classical
firmness of control. It is, in addition, an art of unquestioned
originality.

Our knowledge of Miss Compton-Burnett's life is confined to
a few meager details: "Autobiography is not in my line and my
life has to the outside eye been uneventful."[1] Miss Compton-
Burnett, who was born in London in 1892, is a member of what
her friend Margaret Jourdain once called the "comfortable
classes," or what a later generation would call "The Establish-
ment." Indeed, after seeing a performance of John Osborne's
Look Back in Anger, Ivy Compton-Burnett professed that she
did not understand what the young man was angry about.

She has said to an interviewer, "I do not think I have ever
regarded myself as a professional writer. Even when I was
quite young I always thought I would write. I had a lot of family troubles in my youth and then there was the 1914-18 war,
and a very bad illness which prevented me doing anything
much."[2] She was first tutored at home by brothers who also had
literary ambitions, and she then studied classics at Royal Holloway College of London University.[3]

Dr. Edith Batho, Principal of the College, summarizes her academic career thus:

> Miss Compton-Burnett entered the College in 1902, passed the Intermediate Arts examination in 1903, was awarded a Founder's Scholarship in 1904, and passed the B. A. Honours examination of the University of London in 1906 (Classics, Class II). At that date the Final examinations were held in October, and that may be one of the reasons why she stayed on at the College until the end of the academic session, leaving in 1907.
> The course which she followed involved wide general reading in Latin and Greek as well as closer study of prescribed texts, the study of classical history, philosophy and the Greek drama, and translation unseen from and into both languages.[4]

The set lists of texts she would have studied closely are given in Notes and References in the back of this book.

Her first literary effort, *Dolores* (1911), has not stood the test of time in the author's own judgment. The first mature novel, *Pastors and Masters* (1925), came after the family trouble and the illness. "After the First World War there was a large number of well-off single women. The men they would have married and their well-off brothers had all been killed. It was a manless generation" (Weatherby).

She has traveled a great deal, partly in pursuit of her interest in collecting Alpine wild flowers. "I have had my own flat in London for many years, and for over thirty of them I lived with Margaret Jourdain, the authority on old furniture, who died in April of this year [1951]" (Kunitz).

Miss Compton-Burnett also reads very widely and indicates an interest in all kinds of literature. The only negative judgment she seems to have made is that she finds the Russians nearly impossible to understand, and she wonders about the success of others who claim to understand them. Nevertheless, Chekhov is one of her favorite dramatists. Of more recent authors, she has favorably named Arnold Bennett, Rose Macaulay, Pamela Hansford Johnson, Elizabeth Bowen, Graham Greene, Joyce Cary, P. H. Newby, and L. P. Hartley.

Miss Compton-Burnett writes in longhand. "I do not write slowly or destroy much, but I have long spaces in which I do not write at all. After I finish a book I feel that all the virtue has gone out of me" (Weatherby). She usually plans her books beforehand, because, as she said of a novel she was working on in 1962, "I do not know what is going to happen in it. It is better to start a book with the main line already prepared, but I cannot always do this. I have to start and hope for the best" (Weatherby).

For her achievement as a writer, Ivy Compton-Burnett was made a Commander of the Order of the British Empire in the birthday honors of 1951. She has also received the James Tait Black Memorial Prize in 1956 and was granted an honorary Doctor of Letters degree by the University of Leeds in 1960.

II *Content*

The typical Compton-Burnett novel takes place around the end of the nineteenth century in a country house or a school. A large family, usually dominated by a tyrannical parent, undergoes a cathartic experience of evil—dishonesty, theft, cruelty, adultery, incest, or murder. Since the evil originates within the family and is practiced on other members of the family, it is worked out within the family with no intervention by the law or by the police. Thus there is little occasion for retribution as we ordinarily know it, and moral judgments must be enforced by the individual affected.

The evil itself is rarely dramatized or represented in the course of the work, but the family, pieced out by poor relations and unusually voluble servants, discusses the situation thoroughly in the dining rooms, libraries, gardens, and kitchens. In fact, the novels consist almost exclusively of dialogue; the reader is granted few descriptive details of place, dress, or gesture—he is simply given the age and general appearance of each character on his first introduction. The conversation is as abstractly artificial as that of classical French tragedy, abounding in verbal play, aphorisms, and heavily starched parallelism. But it differs from Racine and Corneille in that its direction and emphasis are frequently comic. Critics have already pointed out close resemblances between some aspects of Miss Compton-Burnett's art and the works of Sophocles, Congreve, Jane Austen, and Henry James; to this list, one must add La Rochefoucauld and Oscar Wilde.

In range, Miss Compton-Burnett's characters cover a span from gurgling two-year-olds to grandfathers in their nineties, with an unusually full complement of persons in their forties and fifties. The families average four children, although several go as high as nine; this number is always supplemented by grandparents, uncles, nephews, aunts, and nieces. The number of single persons—spinsters, bachelors, widows, and widowers —is extremely high; the single men tend to attach themselves to a family, whereas several spinsters often join together to keep a modest home.

The general tenor of her characters' lives results from an economic situation that works in alliance with a peculiarly rural British system of values. Economically, these are landed gentry whose estates do not provide quite enough for them to live in the luxury that a long tradition has established as right for them. As a result, they economize in petty matters, which does little to remedy the situation. The governess teaches the children beyond the usual age for them to have a tutor. Some parents are very sparing with fires in the winter; others serve the children food that the youngsters claim is fit only for ani- mals. Clothes are almost invariably shabby or renovated.

Nearly all the women, and a large number of the men, lead lives of pointless leisure. On the one hand, they often wonder what they do with their time and cannot find a satisfactory answer; on the other hand, when the topic of usefulness is broached, they recoil in strong distaste. They find it inconceiv- able to challenge the idea that inactivity is man's highest state. This standard permeates the whole social fabric, since the servants themselves invariably say that they would prefer an- other station in life, that usefulness is not its own reward, but that some are fated to this condition. Between the extremes of leisure and service are many shades of difference; gentlewomen who have no other support (no close male relation) become governesses or housekeepers, but they are more fortunate if they can be called companions and can command the housekeep- ing unobtrusively. They are always pitied, even by their employers.

Despite the reduced income, the elder son is still considered the most fortunate mortal alive, and his younger brothers are often threatened with talk of the workhouse. For them, education is of primary importance, for a school post is the only gentlemanly alternative, and not a very respectable one at that. Those few sons who are reduced to government jobs in London are ashamed of their fate.

In default of a male heir, there is always a nephew to be groomed for management of the estate. Because of the fortuitousness of his situation, he tends to be edgy; and since he cannot afford to marry, he very often becomes involved in unfortunate liaisons with aunts by marriage or with servants. Whenever possible, this "stumble" is covered by his hasty marriage to a cousin who was being saved for a better match.

This question of sexual passion leads directly into the system of values at the base of these lives. These gentry tend to be Roman in their attitude toward the family as the basis of all common life. Although they often recognize family intercourse to be a chamber of exquisite horrors, they, like all rural persons, see no alternative to it. At its lowest justification, the family is an indispensable convenience; at its highest plane, it is sacred. The frequent occurrence of incest in these novels is a result, in part, of provincialism and rural isolation; at a much deeper level, it is a kind of test situation to measure the strength of the family. This pattern is analogous to that of Roman Catholic novelists who are often said to be obsessed with human situations which test or strain the firmness of Church dogma. The tensions of living with the results of the incest, within a situation of intimate daily contact, constitute the ultimate triumph of family conventions.

If the characters are Roman about the family, they are Greek in their ideas of love. Sexual relations have value only insofar as they produce offspring to carry on the estate. Romantic emotional attachments are a dread disease, closely akin to madness, and are at the base of nearly all crime. Matthew Haslam murders his mother, Sibyl Edgeworth hires a nurse to kill an infant, Josephine Napier kills her niece, and Anna Donne drives an aunt to suicide—all from thwarted or twisted emotional attachments, sometimes strongly allied with greed.

All of the good marriages are based on affection, respect, and convenience; if there is any romantic feeling, it hardly lasts through the honeymoon. Less satisfactory marriages often continue through the forbearance and suppression of feeling. Most

satisfactory marriages are already consummated at the opening
of the novels; presumably happy marriages that are initiated
during the course of the books always occur at the end.

Roger Las Vergnas, one of Miss Compton-Burnett's French
critics, points out that fraternal and amicable feeling is the fundamental cohesive force in this world. It is often true that a
close attachment between two brothers is stronger than the relation of one of the brothers with his wife. Monosexual relations
are frequent in the school milieu.

There subsists throughout this set of values a late Victorian
assumption that men are men, unfortunately, but that women
have fewer sexual drives. If they do not marry early, the men
very often father the illegitimate children of servants or country
girls; a sum of money or a modest provision for life is full payment to the woman, with the illegitimate child becoming a
servant himself, if he is not adopted. Older men whose wives
die are subject to the same compulsions, but they often marry
girls as much as forty years younger than they. Many a plot
grows from the problem of the children's relations with step-
mothers. In only one case is a strong-minded, autocratic wife
found in an extramarital involvement.

Religious faith is restricted on the whole to a few middle-aged
mothers and to their elder daughters. If the family attends
church, it is out of a sense of duty for the example it sets the
lower orders. Family prayers before breakfast are always de-
fended as good for the servants or for someone other than the
speaker; it is nearly always assumed that the person who reads
the service is rendered foolish, and at least one protracted argument centers about who will undertake this unwelcome but
necessary duty. Skepticism is endemic, particularly with the
very old and the very young, with the men, and, at least in one
instance, with the rector himself. Strong religious enthusiasm
on the part of the gentry appears in only one of the mature
novels, and there it is the butt of frequent jokes. The little
faith that exists is in the Established Church; attendance at
chapel is restricted to one or two servants. Conventional observances at weddings and funerals tend to be socially rather
than theologically motivated.

Some of the more indomitable family tyrants conceive of
themselves as nearly equals of the Old Testament deity. One

of them, who has admitted that the idea of the All-Seeing Eye
is of importance only in curbing the savage instincts of children,
has this to say when she is presumed to be mortally ill:

"I don't feel I am going to meet my Maker. And if I were, I
should not fear him. He has not earned the feeling. I almost think
he ought to fear me."

"I think he must," murmured Hugo. "She seems so much her
usual self."[5]

When this grandmother dies, her son carries on in the same pattern, which suggests a Hebraic element to be added to the
Graeco-Roman ones already noted. In such a tribal society, the
patriarch is closely identified with God, and he is the direct
executive on earth of God's will for the tribe. This is made
clear in a blasphemous speech toward the end of the same
novel, of one dependent to another: "' I have never believed in
God. I believe in him now. We have known he is a father. And
I see that he is yours. There are the anger, jealousy, vaingloriousness, vengefulness, love, compassion, infinite power. The
matter is in no doubt'" (231).

The use of the term "tyrant" for the family elder is a habit
probably initiated by Robert Liddell in his book on Ivy Compton-
Burnett. Other critics have objected to this term, with some
cogency, for the elder is not entirely different, morally, spiritually,
or intellectually, from many of the children. He is sometimes
even good enough to show love and compassion as the preceding
quotation indicates. He simply has greater power than the rest.
If others were in his position, many of them would behave
similarly.

The question of who possesses the power is one of chance
—of being male rather than female, or of being born before
another. If the author weights the scales in any one direction,
it is more for the dependent and the female, but not enough to
make the distinction melodramatic. The dependents themselves
are so full of anger, jealousy, vaingloriousness, and vengefulness that the tyrant usually has no choice but to wield the
power for the continuity of the family. To be sure, the habitual
use of power, over a long period, often gives the elderly tyrants
an arbitrary, curt manner, just as it gives the dependents a
cringing, underhanded manner. All this does not mean that

Miss Compton-Burnett erases distinctions between the evil persons and the good ones—they remain one of the firmest categories in her work. And wherever power can be gained outside the conventions of inheritance, it is the evil ones who grasp it.

Those one or two critics who complain that Miss Compton-Burnett shows a weakness in her portrayal of male characters are really objecting simply to the *kinds* of men she treats; her men are completely convincing, but they are leisured country gentlemen, and frequently not very efficient at that. Although they read the London *Times,* they have no relation to Parliament, commerce, or the military. The eccentric rectors of the early novels soon disappear from the works. These country gentlemen are surrounded by large numbers of daughters, sisters, cousins, and aunts. It is hardly surprising that on the whole they show excellent manners, but they tend a bit toward taciturnity, except when they are compulsive talkers. They are a cowed minority within a matriarchal society. At their best, as in the character of Uncle Dudley Gaveston of *A Family and a Fortune* (1939), they are detached but sympathetic and self-sacrificial friends; at next-to-best, they are like Grant Edgeworth of *A House and Its Head* (1935)—poor nephews who are kept in the great house in lieu of a male heir. The nephews are a forbearing lot who, like the uncles, must sacrifice their fiancées, their time, their independence, and whatever else the head of the house demands. The nephews maintain ideal brother-sister relations with their feminine cousins, which are often superior to the relations between real brothers and sisters.

Where there is a male heir, he tends to be the typically overbearing and impatient character; his younger brothers are resentful and usually show fine wit in their acid remarks about their status. The good fathers are mild, subdued creatures like John Ponsonby or Fulbert Sullivan, whose native benevolence shows itself only after the female tyrant is dead or has entirely overreached herself.

The evil men in these novels tend heavily toward self-pity, garrulity, and weakness of character. They are quick to engage themselves to very young women when their wives die or disappear; they mask their selfish motives under the guises of compensation for extreme suffering or neglect. In this syndrome of traits, they are not very different from the grand line of such female tyrants as Sabine Ponsonby, Josephine Napier, Sukey Donne, and Matty Seaton, except that they very seldom show any interest in their children beyond that necessary to enforce household economies. The male tyrants may not lodge themselves in the memory as quite such a cruel and morbid race simply because we expect men to show more taste for domination; what is unusual in them is the traits of whining self-regard and the pose of long-suffering patience usually associated with feminine tyrants.

While all generalizations have weaknesses, they are particularly suspect in dealing with an author of Ivy Compton-Burnett's complexity and specificity of thought. At the best, we can say that the major contrast in her works between male and female tyrants is that each tends to show to a remarkable degree many traits ordinarily associated with the opposite sex. Thus the men, as we have seen, are essentially passive creatures; the tyrannical women are curt, efficient, domineering, and omniscient managers. In fact, even beyond the limited area of tyranny, all of Miss Compton-Burnett's characters show a complexity of mixed sexual traits that recalls many a characterization from Virginia Woolf.

The central faith of these characters is in traditional patterns of behavior and conventions of society as an embodiment of empirical rational judgment that has been proved right by the test of time. Although they do not belong precisely to the class Gray had in mind in the "Elegy Written in a Country Churchyard," they would endorse its sentiments heartily as applying to themselves.

This is a highly conservative, rural society, stiff in its observance of a hierarchy that runs from the master down to the tenant on the male side; and from the mistress on the distaff side down to the under-housemaid and to the *déclassée* country girls who bear the illegitimate children. The most pervasive manifestation of this rank is in forms of address, most of them codified by tradition, as in addressing the governess as "Miss Mitford," but the nursemaid simply as "Bennett." Other forms must be invented to meet new situations; in one of the novels, for example, when a husband remarries, the issue of what his children will call the stepmother becomes a crisis that lasts for many pages. It is a matter of deep importance when young ladies progress in a friendship far enough to use Christian names. Some of the families always call maids and butler's helpers by the name of the first person to hold the position simply because they cannot be bothered to learn the names of new servants.

Within such a social matrix, manners have great importance; for those higher in degree, manners assure continuity and ease of intercourse in a situation where the lower orders would have every reason, without rigid manners, to make trouble. As the author points out, even the Victorian house plan decrees that the highest rooms are reserved for the shortest legs (children) and those least able to mount many steps (servants). On the positive side, good manners show respect for the whole texture of social intercourse, for the rights and privacies of others, and for the prerogatives of sex and age. And such respect is an integral function of benevolence, generosity, and magnanimity.

This statement does not mean, on the other hand, that these novels espouse a priggish set of values; some of the most ill-mannered characters, such as George, the butler's boy in *Bullivant and the Lambs* (1947), speak home truths about the injustice of the social system that are as refreshing as they are cogent. Manners, in short, hold the dialectic together; but, if there were no violation of manners, there would be no dialectic.

At one level, manners are an indication of the individual's surface qualities, but they are also continuous with his deepest spiritual resources. In a very acute sense, crime is only possible to those thieves who do not balk at the deepest invasion of privacy, or to those murderers who callously presume to make for another living individual the most important choice a human being can face. Good manners do not prevent crime, but crime is predicated on bad or false manners.

One of the distinct pleasures of living in such a stable society is the observation of these relationships between outer manner and inner will. Persons of low intelligence and mean spirit in these novels overdo manners to a punctilious comic extreme; tyrants blandly override the conventions when they are sure of their power; evil persons use manners as a mask of inner intention. When Grandmother Ponsonby asks for tea to be served to her alone early in the afternoon, we can be sure that she means to use the hot water to steam open the governess's last letter to her father before it is posted. Josephine Napier, who feels nothing but relief at her husband's death, wears deep mourning to her nephew's wedding because she wants to show the force of her disapproval. Duncan Edgeworth requires his mortally ill wife to preside as usual at breakfast because he cannot conceive of any disturbance to the routine of his day.

Because the good persons in these novels are primarily distinguished by their unobtrusiveness, it is more difficult to isolate their qualities. In addition, they tend always to be in dependent situations, where their manners are given less scope. Since they are outside the primary family power tensions, these governesses, mothers, elder daughters, and bachelor uncles are at their best in informal conversation. Since, as already noted, good manners cannot prevent the occurrence of evil, these characters wield little positive influence over the tyrants. Nevertheless, they usually advise and warn the tyrant of an inappropriate course of behavior—but without effect.

In short, this society possesses many of the typical features of its historical counterpart, but amalgamated into a special aesthetic construct that is peculiar to this author.

III *Technique*

Even though her form and technique reembody the finest achievements of Classical and Neoclassical literary art, Ivy Compton-Burnett has revealed a distinctively personal tone in her novels. Indeed, the fusion of tragic and comic elements in her work defies the easy description of "tragi-comic," for it is entirely unique.

Many readers feel discomfiture when they are confronted by elements that resemble Greek tragedy homogenously blended in the same work with elements that recall Restoration and eighteenth-century comedies of manners. The reason for this discomfiture is that the readers have one set of connotations for tragedy and another for sophisticated comedy, and they have never before associated the one set of connotations with the other. But this association is precisely what makes Miss Compton-Burnett the magnificently original writer that she is.

Marcel Proust—himself a prime example of one who discomfits readers—points out in his aesthetic that remarkably original painters and composers outrage our senses of sight and hearing when we first encounter them, but that, when we accustom ourselves to their idiom, we find ourselves hearing Debussy sounds in nature. This is what Oscar Wilde meant when he remarked that nature began to produce Turner sunsets only after the great artist showed what a sunset could look like. Put simply, the great artist violates our conventional forms of experience by a new stylistic convention which soon takes its place in our apprehension of reality, and we see that all along he was expressing our own deepest experience.

This blend of elements by Miss Compton-Burnett has put many a professional critic on an uncomfortable seesaw; the one who emphasizes the tragic elements in her works says he does so to counteract an overemphasis on the comic; the one who emphasizes the comic says he is compensating for too great an attention to the tragic. Judging from two remarks that occur in *Mother and Son* (1955), we can presume that Ivy Compton-Burnett herself somewhat mistrusts the comic element as an *exclusive* means of representing human experience. Early in the novel, this interchange occurs:

"So it is true that comedy and tragedy are mingled," said Adrian.
"Really it is all tragedy," said his sister. "Comedy is a wicked way of looking at it, when it is not our own."[6]

Later in the book, there is another remark that confirms this view:

". . . Your humour has been bitter, when I thought it was sound?"
"I do not think humour is ever sound. If it is, it is something else." (217)

The very fact that the critical seesaw continues to operate is perhaps the best indication that the blend is composed of nearly equal quantities; but this seeming mistrust of the purely comic as wicked and unsound makes one incline slightly toward the view that Ivy Compton-Burnett's novels are meant as predominantly serious reflections of human experience.

One of the most distinctive qualities of these books is that the author is the most dryly detached of observers, yet her hand is everywhere. Her characters do all the talking, so that she seems to say nothing, and yet she says everything. Wherever cruelty or hypocrisy reveal themselves, it is generally through the speech of the character responsible for the act. All the complex irony of the situation must be identified by the reader from the self-incriminating speeches of the characters. It is almost as if Miss Compton-Burnett attains what the young Stephen Daedalus desires, that the author be like the God of creation, off in a corner paring his fingernails. And yet, the kind of life she treats could only occur, the reader feels, in her novels.

As for the events revealed by the dialogue, these are heavily plotted stories in which the mainsprings of action are passion, property, and power. They employ all the traditional paraphernalia of secret wills, eavesdropping, illegitimacy, and the long-lost letter suddenly discovered in the old desk. While various readers differ in the skill of guessing plots in advance, it is often true that the author inserts enough broad hints to enable the careful reader to sense major occurrences somewhat before they happen. Thus the emphasis is not always on suspense about event; it is often about somewhat more subtle concerns. When will the knowledge of this deed come to light? How many persons will learn of it? Whom will they tell? And, most importantly, what will be the conversational reactions to the event?

Thus dialogue is not just another department of style; it is, rather, the essential medium of expression. The reliance on this form is so complete that we seldom know, except by indications given in the talk of the persons concerned, in which room a conversation is occurring, who is present in the room, or who leaves. Changes from one group of persons to another are not indicated by numbered scenes or stage directions, as in a play, nor is the speaker indicated except where absolutely necessary. Where identifications are unavoidable, Miss Compton-Burnett relies almost entirely on the "John said" formula, and very shortly the repetition becomes so regular as to be unobtrusive. The author obviously has no use for the spurious, awkward variety gained by the "John queried" or "John expostulated" school of dialogue.

The corollaries of this method are many. In the first place, the author herself tells us nothing, as we have already remarked. There is a greater sense of objectivity on her part, and of creation on the reader's part, than is gained by more "directive" writing in which the author points out matters of interest like a tourist guide. When the reader concludes that Maud is a prude or that Lucius is reticent, he has not been told so, he has observed it for himself.

Second, the preponderance of dialogue, with only very rare passages of exposition or soliloquy, makes all the reality social and public. All solitary or private experience comes to the reader by way of the characters' speculation in the teachers' common room, in the kitchen, or in the drawing room. The most frequent occasions for dialogue are meals; at breakfast, luncheon, tea, and dinner, the family gathers, often with large numbers of guests. The large parties sometimes involve every character in the book.

Third, dialogue does not permit any monothematic development of material; regardless of the subject of discussion, there are bound to be from two to ten points of view expressed in rapid succession, many of them tossing the reader from one attitude to its extreme opposite and back again. This dialectic is far more complex in its operations than the Platonic or the Hegelian varieties; what saves it from impossible complexity is that the subject of conversation is a universal truth about time, age, death, sex differences, marriage, self-interest, or money. The range of subjects is almost identical with that of a classical aphorist like La Rochefoucauld, except that sexual passion is not analyzed to the same extent. This concern with universal truths shades off into clichés, truisms, and platitudes; these are often thrown up like a shuttlecock, to be batted back and forth by the speakers.

At the simplest level, the opening platitude may be a proverb or a scrap of folk wisdom which the speaker himself destroys: " '. . . So perhaps it is all for the best. That is always said when things are particularly bad, so there could hardly be a better occasion for saying it.' "[7] Sometimes a second speaker punctures the platitude:

". . . It never rains but it pours."
"I think it nearly always rains. We only notice it when it pours." (*Family*, 258)

A longer example follows in which the destruction of the platitude is an extended and complex process involving many shifting values:

"Ridley was always a very masculine type," said Faith. "And he was some years older than I was, and I think more developed for his age."

"You must remember you are speaking of your brother, dear," said Hope.

"I said nothing against him, Mother."

"You were damning him with faint praise; I think with almost no praise at all. I believe you were just damning him."

"I am not always thinking of praising people or not praising them."

"It would be nice to think of the first, dear."

"You don't often do it yourself, Mother."

"Well, I so seldom see any cause for praise. And when I do, I am so often upset about it. So it is not very easy for me."[8]

When the platitude is a religious or literary allusion, it is generally to the Bible, the Book of Common Prayer, or to such familiar tags as "To thine own self be true" or "Nature red in tooth and claw."

Henry James has a similar habit of using clichés, but of revivifying them by having a second person or the narrator take them in their root meaning, the one they had before overuse stifled their power. If one character, for example, says "Now the fat is in the fire," another is sure to warn him to stand back from the sparks. Ivy Compton-Burnett works a slight variation on this device, as one of her critics has remarked. Whenever a character opens a statement with the cliché locution "I'm afraid," as in "I'm afraid I lost my glove," the answerer takes up the question of fear very seriously, rather than the idea of loss:

"I always say there is something fine running through Aunt Eliza," said Constance.

"I am glad I do not hear you," said Malcolm.[9]

A variation is the figurative question which receives a literal answer:

". . . Hengist, how often have I told you not to keep your hands in your pockets?"

"I have not counted, Grandma," said the latter, too politely to incur rebuke. (*Mighty*, 12)

As Miss Compton-Burnett has remarked, the greatest difficulty in her style is its extreme condensation; she might have added that abstraction plays its part too. A good sample is a very long dialectical colloquy on the nature of "real worth" which is in itself a very abstract subject. While the pronoun reference is clear to the very attentive reader, those with less patience and application become easily lost in the thicket:

"I dislike this mockery of real worth. Nothing else counts."

"That is surely not true," said Emma. "Many things count."

"Does nothing count without it?" said Sir Ransom. "May that be said?"

"It makes things count more," said Selina. "I know, because I am not supposed to have it. And it makes people very mean about everything else."

"It may have to count by itself," said Emma.

"And surely may do so," said Edmund.

"Oh, no one would admit having it by itself," said Bridget. "People do not count it as much as that. They admire things that are of more advantage to the possessor. Worth is of more to other people. But I daresay it is too rare for any of it to matter much."

"Is it so rare?" said Emma.

"Well, of course there is good in everyone. But we are told about it too often. It suggests it is little enough to be overlooked."

"It has been overlooked in my case," said Selina. "But I have never made the most of it. I somehow feel I should have scorned to do so."

"You would not have made so little of your other advantages," said Gaunt. "People dispense with worth most easily. They would not acquiesce in being thought ordinary or ungifted."

"Of course not, when they would not know they were," said Bridget. "It is only their hearts that they know. Their worth is the thing they can judge of."

"I do not mind saying I am both those things," said Anne.

"And you count indeed, Miss Anne," said Mildred, coming through the room to replace the teapot by another. "We do not know anyone who counts more in her own way."

"I fear that proves I am both."[10]

Since the author uses so few other resources, dialogue also must carry the burden of characterization. As in Shakespeare, all the characters seem to talk alike (within the conventions of the style) with faultless grammar (regardless of social level), accuracy, concision, point, and a slight tendency toward abstraction. Bores and fools tend to talk too much and almost invariably about themselves; they try hard to make their motives appear in the best light, but their very preoccupation with

self is automatic condemnation. Certain petty characters have
a deadly addiction to cliché. When very young children appear,
they break none of the dialogue conventions, but their speech
is geared with remarkable accuracy to the age level at which
children refuse to talk in company, talk only in questions, or
gush about family concerns to outsiders. Miss Compton-Burnett's
children are on the whole so wise, however, that we very seldom
encounter the empty babbler at that level, although he appears
among the adults. Servants in the range of butlers, cooks, and
housekeepers speak with a formal rigidity impossible even to
their employers. The only slang occurs, and then very rarely,
in the mouths of adolescent male servants.

Robert Liddell, who has made a beginning at classifying the
many kinds of Compton-Burnett speeches, argues convincingly
that many of the rapid-fire, one-line trains of speeches owe
something to the stichomythia of Greek tragedy. On the other
hand, there are also rather long, set speeches of a nearly ora-
torical character, the most remarkable being that of Hetta
Ponsonby in *Daughters and Sons* (1937) which we shall discuss
in the treatment of that novel.

While this is not the place for an exhaustive catalog of types
of speeches we might note one or two of the more remarkable varieties of recurrent patterns. Perhaps the most delightful of all
is the halting, "foot in mouth" variety in which a character tries
to thank a doctor who treated a patient that died: "'Dr. Smollet,'
said Dulcia, 'we have thanked the rector for what he has done,
thanked him in all sincerity. And no one has made any movement of thanking you, a condition which I would remedy. We
are grateful from our hearts for what you have done, tried to
do'—Dulcia was hampered by the climax of Ellen's illness—'for
doing all for Mrs. Edgeworth that was humanly possible.'"[11]

In a second example, Miss Seymour tries to express her
gratitude for a dinner to a host whose mother died in the course
of the meal, and whose family engaged in airing dirty linen:
"'It is time for us to go. We have had a lovely evening; I
mean, we have enjoyed it all so much; I mean, we have been
so glad to be at your side through everything. And of course
there has been nothing. Except, of course, that Mrs. Ponsonby's
death has been everything. Stephen, it is a time for you to speak.
People of rare words always do the best. It is like rare smiles.'"[12]

A second variety, all the more refreshing in an artificially formal society, is the "plain talk" speech, usually motivated by anger, in which one of the victims talks back to the tyrant in a devastatingly simple accusation:

"Mother, I don't know if you realise in what an inconceivably senseless way you are behaving. I can only hope you don't, for the sake of your respect for yourself, and our respect for you. Do you think it an advantage to estrange your husband and family, and go your way with nothing in your life but deeper sinking into selfish bitterness? We shall not alter our lives and aims for the whims of one woman. You may have your opinions. We have ours. We show extreme forbearance to your weakness, as if you look at things straight, you cannot but see. You have an excellent husband, dutiful sons, and a daughter who could only be a pleasure to a woman with the feelings of a mother. We have not spoken before; I am not going to speak any longer now. But if you do not pull yourself up in time, you will find yourself one day a very lonely old woman."[13]

Finally, Miss Compton-Burnett compensates for the absence of stream of consciousness in her novels by making the overt speeches of the characters cover an astonishing range of degrees of intention on the part of the speakers and by having an equal variety in the degrees of reception on the part of the auditors. Many persons enter a room suddenly, only to hear slander of themselves or others. Other characters read or doze on sofas in dimly-lit libraries, where they overhear intimate revelations not meant for their ears. In other cases, children or dependents make corrosive *sotto voce* comments that are picked up by the tyrants; even within this convention, one sometimes wonders how innocent the speakers are. At large dinners, a small family group discusses private concerns at one corner of the table, with the guests discussing their delight at being treated to such a spectacle. Characters who appear to have left the room linger at the door to catch judgments of themselves. The eavesdropping reaches such proportions in the school scenes of *Two Worlds and Their Ways* (1949) that one of the children remarks "'This place is a nest of professional eavesdroppers,'" and is overheard saying that! In short, Miss Compton-Burnett uses all the stage tricks of entrance and exit, asides, eavesdropping, and varying degrees of audibility even more flexibly and tellingly than could be managed in the theater.

Although she has not commented directly about this technique, it is clear that Miss Compton-Burnett's use of dialogue has a nearly metaphysical significance within the aesthetic world she creates. Since her whole art consists of people talking, there are no moral or social judgments exterior to the persons in her world. She nevertheless gains the immediacy of experience of Henry James's celebrated point-of-view method without all the heavy burden of introspection which James's technique entails. Her emphasis on the social and the public does not run the danger of fatuous extroversion; there are many richly individual eccentrics and deviates within her work, none of whom is judged by conformist standards. Each person is what he is, and he is judged by his fellows according to a wide variety of standards.

IV *Literary Values*

As Pamela Hansford Johnson points out in her pamphlet on Ivy Compton-Burnett, the greater proportion of criticism has been highly laudatory. The early enthusiasm was expressed by a rather sophisticated coterie of professional reviewers and literary specialists, but adverse criticism has increased somewhat with the author's widening audience. While the final chapter of this book will be devoted to a detailed view of the criticism, it will be well at this point to survey some of the general objections to her novels and to glance at other kinds of critical comments in order to arrive at a clearer view of the positive literary values of the work.

While many of the objections which have appeared must be considered as referring to possible weaknesses, we must recognize that any aesthetic commitment to one course of action invariably entails rejection of other possible courses of action; consequently, these weaknesses have to be seen in the light of the positive choices that necessitate them.

At the outset, we can dismiss those objections which refer to Miss Compton-Burnett's preference for a past era and for somber material; as Henry James pointed out in "The Art of Fiction," we must give the author his choice of subject matter. If we object to the content, we may do so on a personal basis, but we are hardly making a rational judgment about the art. From her own point of view, the author has commented on these objections in the following terms: "I do not feel that I have any real or organic knowledge of life later than about 1910. I should not write of later times with enough grasp or confidence."[14] In a recent interview, Miss Compton-Burnett remarked that she wishes to deal with a permanent set of human values, and that the flux of contemporary life obscures many a writer's vision of these values. Of a corollary objection that the novels do not deal with life as we know it, she says: "I think that actual life supplies a writer with characters much less than is thought. . . . And people in life hardly seem to be definite enough to appear in print. They are not good enough or bad enough, or clever or stupid enough, or comic or pitiful enough. . . . As regards plot I find real life no help at all. Real life seems to have no plots. And as I think a plot desirable and almost necessary, I have this extra grudge against life" (*Orion*, 25).

Again, largely in response to reviewers' and critics' remarks, Miss Compton-Burnett indicates that she feels no need for exposition and description since plays, which dispense with these elements, are also treatments of imaginary human beings and their lives. "I think that my writing does not seem to be as 'stylized' as it apparently is, though I do not attempt to make my characters use the words of actual life. I cannot tell you why I write as I do, as I do not know. I have even tried not to do it, but find myself falling back into my own way" (*Orion*, 21).

Since Miss Compton-Burnett has commented rather directly on the influences and resemblances attributed to her work by reviewers, it is just as well to have her word on these matters:

I have read Jane Austen so much, and with such enjoyment and admiration, that I may have absorbed things from her unconsciously. I do not think myself that I have any real likeness to her. I think that there is possibly some likeness between our minds. (*Orion*, 21)

. . . .

I am not a great reader of Henry James. . . . I enjoy him less than many other writers. He does not reveal as much as I should like of the relations of his characters with each other. And I am surprised if my style is as intricate as his. I should have thought it was only rather condensed. If it is, I sympathise with the people who cannot read my books. (*Orion*, 22)

. . . .

My Own Way

The Greek dramatists I read as a girl, as I was classically educated and read them with the attention to each line necessitated by the state of my scholarship; and it is difficult to say how much soaked in, but I should think very likely something. I have not read them for many years—another result of the state of my scholarship. (*Orion*, 23)

Another charge brought against Ivy Compton-Burnett is that of sameness. Aside from Robert Liddell, who is a most devoted admirer, most critics admit that they have great difficulty distinguishing in their memories between plots and characters in the various novels because each one resembles the others so closely. This is true; but one must grant Liddell his point that if one reads the novels with very close attention, he will discover an astonishing variety of nuances. It is simply a question of how concentratedly the reader wishes to focus his attention. Miss Compton-Burnett is most decidedly not writing for an audience drugged by the passive habits of electronic and televisual communication.

No one doubts that her books are difficult to read, for the dialogue is tightly condensed and every word must be weighed judiciously. But the books are not obscure. The language is parsimoniously simple, with a monosyllabic emphasis. The sentences, aside from the intricacy of parallel structure, are also quite straightforward. Thus the reader encounters none of the verbal ornateness of Faulkner nor the syntactical complexity of James. And, unlike nearly all of her contemporaries, Miss Compton-Burnett is completely free of symbolic and figurative meanings. She also avoids that other major cause of obscurity in twentieth-century literature—the habit of allusion to arcane literary forbears. Indeed, in everything but the complex rational thought behind it, the writing is extremely simple. This trait, to say the least, is refreshing in our day. The only other writer to equal the disarming surface simplicity of Miss Compton-Burnett's style is perhaps Gertrude Stein, who has other kinds of complexities behind the bland facade.

Other critics have attacked Miss Compton-Burnett's choice of "melodramatic" plot structure—even to the point of calling her lazy. She is accused of shoddy artistic carpentry because the events seem to occur arbitrarily, without sufficient justification, preparation, or motivation.

At the outset, critics fail to realize that she is not attempting to write the standard realistic kind of novel in which the author is constantly apologizing for telling a story by trying to make it seem "lifelike." But as Mme. Nathalie Sarraute points out in some of her more trenchant criticism of the modern novel, these "lifelike" details are themselves highly artificial conventions which have become so worn and familiar as to be useless. And we have certainly had an example in Bertolt Brecht's dramaturgy of an author who constantly jolts his audience to prevent it from becoming absorbed into a dreamlike trance; he wants it to know each moment it is in the theater that it has consciously chosen to be entertained, and that it is there to hear a story, not to fool itself into thinking it is experiencing "life."

The basis of all literary appeal from the very beginning has been the excitement of a surprising, absorbing narrative. To the degree that melodrama deals in high excitement and suspense, it directly satisfies basic literary needs. Melodrama gets a bad name when it carries the devices of surprise and shock beyond any acceptable criterion of aesthetic credibility; in so doing it also often divorces the narrative from the kind of human wisdom that grows out of a balanced contemplation of the significance of events. A work of art rises above shoddy melodrama when moral value and subtlety of response emerge from the immediate shock of the event.

Miss Compton-Burnett *does* relate a rousingly exciting yarn, and in doing this she often carries the shock of coincidence right up to the edge of aesthetic credibility—and far beyond any standard applicable to the Realistic novel. But the rich justification for this excess is the incredibly complex, delicate, and balanced conversational reaction to event on the parts of the characters. She usually conveys the immediate shock of occurrence rapidly and baldly, and then the seasoned reader, glad to have the theme of the movement stated, settles back for the delicious development and variations of the theme in the ensuing conversations.

We are a generation conditioned by the downright hostility to plot that was made fashionable by Chekhov, Katherine Mansfield, Virginia Woolf, and James Joyce. But there are many indications that the era of experimentation with plotless fiction is at an end, interesting as it was. And the popularity of Miss Compton-Burnett's work is one of these signs.

As we shall see in the discussion of *Elders and Betters* (1944), it is popular in some quarters to refer to Miss Compton-Burnett as an amoral writer who recognizes only the law of the jungle. This widespread fallacy is based on the fact that many of the evil actions in her books are not legally definable as crimes; and, even when they are, the evildoer almost always gains his end and lives very happily with the fruits of his effort. Miss Compton-Burnett is asserting that human cruelty goes deeper than the law can penetrate and ranges farther than the police can discover. She simply forbids the facile consolation of saying that strong laws deter crime and that Scotland Yard always gets its man. But even beyond these moral clichés in the civil sphere, she refuses to resort to the possibly callous assumption that the undiscovered murderer or thief will be punished by God—or by psychological mechanism—through the madness of unbearable guilt. In one sense, Miss Compton-Burnett's vision is far more obdurate than that of the Book of Job, where inconceivably harsh injustice is explained by the Voice from the Whirlwind which states, in essence, that man is too petty to understand God's moral order. She also goes farther than the Greeks in her refusal to assume a moral order in the universe.

What she does believe is that morality is a human invention —a result of empirical reasoning—and that, like all human standards, it is observed by decent persons and violated by the indecent ones. All adults understand that adultery is wrong, but this understanding does not always control their actions. She uncompromisingly states that the evil man gets away with what he can get away with. If Miss Compton-Burnett has blasted the whole convention of poetic justice in literature, the action has about it an honesty unique in the history of literature.

We are not safe in assuming that the supposed harshness of her view argues in her a frivolous or a perverse spirit. It is much more logical to assume that she has been favored with a moral vision of unrivaled clarity and probity, and that her refusal to countenance the superficial apologetics of standard morality is an act of courage, motivated by a tenderness of concern for human suffering that is beyond the scope of our most vocal professional moralizers.

Miss Compton-Burnett's distinctive approach to moral values is complexly rational, but it leads her to a detached, balanced, and rarefied chastity of moral vision that is paralleled only by the mystics who have arrived at their insights by totally different paths. If evil is as pervasive and virulent as this, and if it is inextricably allied to good, then we must learn to sit down to breakfast with it, to cuddle it in the nursery, to feel it beside us in the night, and to accommodate it in our hearts.

Miss Compton-Burnett has chosen an art of severe limitation and restriction, as is always true of the Classicist; the narrow compass gained thereby gives the work high intensity and hard polish. If these qualities are cherished, then the reader must also accept the fact that something must be sacrificed to gain this tightness. Her commitment to the dialogue novel, for example, gives her a medium that is sensitive, highly responsive to control, ordered, neat, and subtle; but this concentration rules out representation of interior monologue, subconscious motivation, and reverie. If we take up the implications of the intensity and the polish, we can liken her art to that of carving precious stones: the work is detailed, controlled, enduring, and valuable; but, in the very attainment of these qualities, it must sacrifice what could be gained by working in clay.

For what it attempts to do, Miss Compton-Burnett's art is perfect; and, as Virginia Woolf once remarked of Addison, who is to say that one perfect drop of water is not as satisfying in itself as the whole Thames? Moreover, Miss Compton-Burnett's kind of perfection entails an absorbingly exciting narrative of august passions and unspeakable crimes, refracted through the elegant wit of the comedy of manners. This peculiar combination enables her to attain a unique moral vision that combines the tragic irony of Greek drama with the surface arabesques of Restoration comedy. Hers is an art of sophistication above all else.

CHAPTER 2

Good is Bad Condensed

> ". . . good is bad condensed . . . and holds
> more bad than anything else. . . ."
>
> —*Pastors and Masters*

I *Matriarchs and Murder*

AFTER a tentative beginning with *Dolores,* Miss Compton-Burnett's mature work is initiated by *Pastors and Masters,* a short and rather sketchy work; it is the first of the school novels, and the work which also introduces the first fullfledged family tyrant. *Brothers and Sisters* (1929) opens the line of the manor novels and offers a feminine variation on the tyrant. As if this volume had exhausted for a time the strain of high comedy that distinguishes its best scenes, the next three novels—*Men and Wives* (1931), *More Women than Men* (1933), and *A House and Its Head* (1935)—introduce the most somber passage in the author's works. For one thing, they all share murder within the family as a plot situation. With the possible exception of *Elders and Betters* (where Anna Donne drives her aunt to suicide through psychological insinuations), Miss Compton-Burnett has never returned to this device in her later works. In addition, *Brothers and Sisters* and the two succeeding volumes present an impressive line of indomitable matriarchal tyrants that remain among the author's most memorable characters.

II *Dolores*

Miss Compton-Burnett says of her first novel, "to my mind 'Dolores' [1911] is a piece of juvenilia and has no interest. Also a brother interfered with it, and made it less my own."[1] Although she would prefer that it be ignored, it is a fascinating, even a moving, book for readers who know her later novels—if one overlooks the youthful gaucheries of style.

Dolores is separated from the mature books by fourteen years, by a revolution in narrative approach, and by a shifting of values. Nevertheless many of the later mannerisms are here in embryo, particularly in the stiletto thrusts of Elsa Blackwell's cynical remarks and in names like Perdita, Felicia, Sigismund, and Bertram.

The narrative method is heavily expository, with extremely condensed, awkward sentences which one assumes are misprints at first reading. The intense condensation of meaning is largely attained by syntactical ellipsis and by ruthless, polysyllabic abstraction of diction—both of them excesses of intelligence. Especially at the outset, the author is given to elaborately arch rhetorical questions. Perhaps it is a matter of becoming accustomed to these conventions, but the later chapters seem to approach the mature manner much more closely.

The novel contains realistic observations and settings, and much of the effort is directed at accurate portrayal of village relations between a typical rector of the Established Church, a Methodist temperance lecturer, and a Fundamentalist, each of whose families support the father's attitude. The dialogue is exact in the reproduction of individual speech habits and eccentricities, as no later Compton-Burnett dialogue could conceivably be.

Dr. Edith Batho adds that a copy of *Dolores* in the Royal Holloway College library contains notes made and verified by contemporaries, indicating that most of the senior lecturers who appear in the college scenes of the novel bear close resemblance to lecturers at Royal Holloway at the time of Ivy Compton-Burnett's attendance.[2] Miss Compton-Burnett herself explicitly denies any resemblance between the characters of this novel and actual persons.

Pamela Hansford Johnson has noted parallels between this book and George Eliot's *Middlemarch,* as well as with Brontë novels. Dolores is an intelligent and forceful young lady who throws herself into an absolute, unquestioning orgy of self-sacrifice. She renounces a post at her college in order to tutor her younger half brother and sisters at the insistence of her stepmother, Sophia Hutton, who is an early adumbration of the matriarchal tyranny we shall encounter later in Sophia Stace. Then she steps aside to allow an unworthy friend to marry

Sigismund Claverhouse, an elderly, blind playwright with whom Dolores has an intense spiritual identification. Later, she gives up the love of William Soulsby, intimate companion of Sigismund, to her half sister Sophy, out of pure, self-lacerating kindness. Her fourth great sacrifice is in returning to her father after Sigismund, now a lonely, bereft widower, realizes the force of her devotion. When Sigismund is dying, Dolores's father keeps her away from Sigismund just long enough to prevent her from consoling the dying man. Then, showing how lightly he values the sacrifice his daughter made to stay with him, Dolores's father quickly remarries.

All of Dolores's sacrifices are free choices, made in agonizingly full consciousness of the price. It is simply taken for granted that her stepmother, father, brother, and half sister have a greater need—because they are either older or crueler, or younger or gentler. It makes little sense, except that Dolores's unquestioning capacity for renunciation is found to be convenient for others.

It is ironical, in its way, that the only great call on Dolores outside the family is for self-abnegation before the needs of a blind old playwright. Thus the poignancy of her sacrifices to the family is simply that they prevent her from making an even greater extrafamilial sacrifice.

Miss Hansford Johnson is right in saying that, in contrast to the values of *Dolores,* all of the later novels deal in one way or another with the futility and fatuousness of self-sacrifice. But none of them has this heroine-centered construction; therefore, the question does not really arise in the same terms. *Dolores* is rather like the later novels in that most of the sacrifices do the recipients little good, and they are not rewarding to the person who makes the gift. The only substantial difference is that in the later novels Dolores herself has disappeared, and with her the whole question of willing, conscious renunciation of personal advantage.

III Pastors and Masters

As far as the author is concerned, she says "I always see 'Pastors and Masters' as my first book. The long interval between them [*Dolores* and *Pastors and Masters*] was the result of family troubles and a period of ill health, and has no literary significance."[3]

In the seven short chapters of *Pastors and Masters* (1925), Miss Compton-Burnett hits her characteristic stride; it is difficult to imagine how the first readers took this book, but for those who know the later achievements, the pages are rich with promise. Looking at the book on its own merits, one finds the weakness of the plot is somewhat compensated for by richness of characterization through dialogue.

At the center of the narrative are Nicholas and Emily Herrick, half brother and sister, the fainéant owners of a boys' school, whose elegant leisure is gained at the expense of the bedraggled Mr. and Mrs. Merry, who have few qualifications for the journeyman work they do. The other two teachers, Mr. Burgess and Miss Basden, parallel the Herricks and the Merrys; Mr. Burgess is a showpiece because he has the degree Mr. Merry lacks, but Miss Basden does all the work. The other two masters are Richard Bumpus and William Masson, two dons at the local university. Although there is always talk of Emily Herrick marrying Masson, everyone seems to understand that he is far too happy in his lifelong intimacy with Bumpus to consider matrimony.

The pastors of the title, the Reverend Peter Fletcher and his nephew Francis and the Reverend Henry Bentley, are not closely involved in the plot. They seem somehow left over from *Dolores*. The Fletchers are simply a convenient soundingboard of orthodox doctrine against which to bounce the freely and somberly pagan pronouncements of the Herricks. The Reverend Henry Bentley, who appears simply because his sons study at the Herrick school, provides a masterful foretaste of the typical Compton-Burnett family tyrant. He speaks at length, but only to carp about remarks or actions of others, to find fault, and to upbraid his minions for their enforced silence. For the rest, he continues an endless lament about his self-sacrifice to an ungrateful, unmannered, undistinguished family. In her concern for her half brothers, his daughter Delia forecasts many good daughters in the later novels.

The plot develops around the theft by Nicholas Herrick of a manuscript written by Bumpus. Herrick assumes it to be the work of a recently deceased master and passes it off as his own. Through a complicated set of circumstances, Bumpus is prevented from exposing Herrick because some of his own double-dealing would therefore come to light.

Throughout the novel there has been an obsessive concern in most of the conversations with the relative merits of men and women; in a tête-à-tête following the literary evening at which both Herrick and Bumpus were to read their identical manuscripts, Emily reveals to Peter's wife, Theresa Fletcher, that she understands the deviousness of the men. She does not reveal her discovery to them, however, since each of the men is so entirely caught up in his own egotism.

As the novel ends, it is clear that the men will continue to lord it over the women; that the Herricks will continue in their unmerited leisure; that the Merrys will continue to bully the boys for their own lack of status; that the Reverend Bentley will do the same service for his family; and that each person will simply live on with a deeper knowledge of the others' failings. If this sounds like a failure to resolve issues, it is really the result of a moral vision which is clear in this summary speech, in which Nicholas Herrick replies to a character who remarks that he yields rather easily to impatience: " 'Patience contains more impatience than anything else, as I judge. . . . Think how it is with everything; how tolerance, for example, is only condensed intolerance, and how it holds more intolerance than anything else. It is just a case for intolerance to be kept in. And think how religion holds more dislike of religion than anything else!' "

And it is Emily Herrick who adds the capstone: " 'I think that good is bad condensed . . . and holds more bad than anything else. . . .' "[4] Thus the sense of stasis in the resolution of the plot is in reality a tense balance between conflicting moral tendencies.

IV Brothers and Sisters

Brothers and Sisters (1929) is an incredibly rich confirmation of the promises inherent in the earlier work; it is with this novel that Miss Compton-Burnett reaches a plateau of high quality which sets a challenging, self-imposed standard for later works. The major gain is that the interest of the plot is apparent at the outset; it is smoothly carried through several major crises, any one of which would have served to blast *Pastors and Masters* to bits. But of even greater importance is the manner in which the characters are integrated into the action so that each of them has a functional significance. The very effectiveness of this technical brilliance guarantees that the author's moral insight is given movingly full expression. In addition, the book shows a smooth advancement in the author's command of a large cast of characters; six pairs of brothers and sisters, all articulate and perceptive persons, provide a wide variety of ironic contrasts in their symmetrical groupings and regroupings.

The plot concerns Christian and Sophia Stace, who have married despite the objection of the latter's father, Andrew Stace. Since Christian is an adopted son, Sophia can see no bar to the union; and she fails to reveal that her father left in a desk a secret document to be opened on his death. Twenty-five years later, after they have had three children, it gradually comes to light that they are actually half brother and sister.

The full-blown portent of Miss Compton-Burnett's mixture of tragic and comic elements is most apparent in this third novel. Although there are enough engagements at the end to provide "happy endings" for four conventional novels, the pairings are determined by Christian and Sophia's violation of one of civilized man's most deeply felt taboos. Obtuseness, self-seeking, arrogance, hypocrisy, and secretiveness have preceded the happy marriages.

This mixed content is presented in a mixed style, since there is a strong element of Congreve and Wilde even at the most hideously dolorous of crises. As an example, let us take the first meeting of Gilbert and Caroline Lang with Andrew and Dinah Stace after they have learned that their respective engagements must be broken. Not only are Andrew and Dinah the children of an incestuous union, but Gilbert and Caroline, to whom they are engaged, are their uncle and aunt. Andrew and Dinah are walking down the stairs with their brother Robin as Gilbert and Caroline Lang come toward them. Dinah speaks first:

"Well if we are equal to this occasion, no other in our lives can find us at a loss. We may look forward to all emergencies without misgiving."

"You may," said Caroline. "To speak at this moment and in that spirit! It is a great word and a great deed!"

"Did you compose it in your mind before?" said Robin.

"As Caroline and Gilbert came up the stairs," said Dinah.

"Then the act was immense," said Robin. "To say what you planned before, when the time for it came! Has any one ever done that? Can anything in life get the upper hand of you?"

Good Is Bad Condensed

"No, I said it could not," said Dinah.

"The circumstances are perhaps an unusual stimulus," said Andrew. "Not that I seem to find them so myself."[5]

The most obvious way of accounting for the comedy is to attribute it to the high intelligence with which the entire novel is conceived and executed. When any situation at all is viewed from such a vantage point, and especially when it deals with the social life of sixteen important characters, complex contradictions and ironies are inevitable. Such intelligence does not, as is often assumed, rule out profundity and warmth of sympathy; conversely, we might say that the very complexity of the judgments in this novel stems from the intimacy of the author's identification with each of the characters in turn.

Mere simplemindedness, such as is revealed in the ingenuous stupidities of Tilly Bateman, excuses itself by the tenderness with which the other characters and the reader regard her; the helpless frustration of her brother Latimer at his father Peter's incredible social gaucheries elicits a reaction more suitable to his male dilemma; whereas the nearly vicious stupidity of his father earns him the kind of edgy resentment which he is constitutionally unable to understand. The rector and his sister, Edward and Judith Dryden, are dealt with a bit summarily because, in their willful determination to reshape reality according to a sweetminded but pale ideal, they reveal a weakness that makes them essentially dull persons. Julian Wake is a glittering, gossipy dragonfly; although his interests are strongly allied with those of Peter, his style exalts him to a level where what was harmful in Peter's gossip is here highly entertaining.

It is with Sophia Stace, the first richly developed tyrant, that we see the full scope of the author's human understanding. If she has indirectly killed her half brother-husband and stained the lives of her children (not only by their guilty inheritance, but by incautiously revealing the secret to Peter, and thus making life in the village impossible for them) many of these consequences could hardly be the results of conscious viciousness. The root of the whole problem was her refusal to look at the secret document in her father's desk because of her fear that it was a will which would disinherit her.

There is something fiendish about Sophia's propensity for breakfast crises; it is as if she could not start early enough in

[45]

the day to exercise her power. The following is a typical instance of her full display; it follows the death of her husband, before whom she did not reveal all her lust for control:

"We are not a cheerful party, are we?" she said.
There was no reply.
"We are not a cheerful party, are we?"
"No, we are not," said Robin. "We have not much reason to be."
"Are we?" said Sophia, looking at Andrew and Dinah.
"No," said Andrew.
"Can you only speak in monosyllables, my son?"
"Nothing more was needed then," said Andrew.
"Oh, I don't know," said Sophia. "I don't think you all ought to sit, dreary and monosyllabic, and make no effort at intercourse, just because your mother is in great sadness and loneliness of heart, and never spare her an encouraging word. When my life is broken, I don't want less from people who are supposd to love me. I need more."
"You exact too much from people in that position," said Andrew. "You have gone too far."
"Oh, do I? Well, I don't get it then," said Sophia. "I don't know what I have had, I am sure, to be taken so much into account."
There was silence.
"What do I get?" said Sophia. "What do I have, Andrew? It was you who spoke of my wanting too much."
"Andrew did not say you had it. He said you claimed it," said Dinah, trying to speak lightly. "We all find that difference." (178)

Earlier, Dinah has remarked, " 'Power has never been any advantage to Sophia. . . . It has worn her out, and every one who would have served her' " (182). As a result, the children know, on her death, how to summarize the matter: "The survey of Sophia's life flashed on them, the years of ruthlessness and tragedy, power and grief. Happiness, of which she was held to have had so much, had never been real to Sophia. They saw it now" (239).

V   Men and Wives

Ivy Compton-Burnett's next novel, *Men and Wives* (1931), ends on a different note; Harriet Haslam, the mother-tyrant, is given this parting word by a friend: " 'Harriet was always a fortunate woman' " (278). She is fortunate in the way that a tyrant wishes to be—in a way that even Sophia Stace could not have envisioned. Not only does Harriet cow the will of her victims, but she also makes them positively work in her cause; and her death is poignantly regretted all around. In contrast to the previous novels, *Men and Wives* is a somber, nearly harrowing work that evokes feelings much closer to the classic terror and pity than any of the others. The comic effects are more sharply ironical and stained with melancholy. There is far greater emphasis on breakfast scenes in which the dark and distraught Lady Haslam appears, worn with sleepless nights, to harry her eloquently rebellious children.

She wishes each of them to renounce the course of action closest to his heart; the pattern of Harriet's requirements has its source in the same fierce religious drive that motivated the elder Andrew Stace of *Brothers and Sisters*: one must be earnest and practical in order to be respectable, despite the fact that this usually means one must resign oneself to petty slavery for the advantage of others. The battle shapes up most intensely with the eldest son, Matthew, who wishes to marry Camilla Bellamy, the divorced wife of the rector. Shortly after the impassioned speech of Matthew's (quoted above in Chapter 1), Lady Harriet Haslam fails at an attempted suicide, an attempt which she regrets having made. After a period in a mental institution, she returns to snap the whip even more sharply at the family that has relaxed during her absence. In what appears to be her second attempt at suicide, she is successful; shortly afterward, however, Matthew confesses that he put a poison tablet among her sleeping pills. The doctor and the family quickly cover up the incident as a mental delusion of Matthew's, for he has obviously inherited his mother's mental infirmities. But the village will rumble for several generations.

Although the "Freudianizing" critics seem not to have discovered these novels yet, one can see the fertile field open before them in this work. All of Harriet Haslam's struggles with her children have a faintly Jocastan element. At her bedroom door, moments before she takes the poison Matthew has prepared for her, she pleads with her son to postpone his marriage simply to please her—and she rather remarkably adds that she makes the request because she knows she has not heretofore merited his love. Although his sexual drive is absolutely frustrated, Matthew retaliates fiercely; Gregory, the youngest son, is in the opposite situation. In his intense devotion to Harriet, his shame-

less need to sit at the feet of all the elderly ladies in the neighborhood, to go out with the ladies after dinner, and to attend
gossipy sewing parties, he reveals a classic case of arrested sexual
development. While these elements exist in the work, one hopes
that the "Freudianizers" will continue to ignore them, since all
Freudian theory—literary as well as clinical—is tinged with
ameliorative therapy, which is totally irrelevant to Miss Compton-
Burnett's world view. In addition, nearly all Freudian literary
analysis leans to symbolic interpretations which would also seriously distort the author's method.

In her continuing comment on the nature of power, Ivy
Compton-Burnett has in *Men and Wives* allied the exercise of
domination with insanity and murder; this is simply a deepening
of the tragic concern with incest in the preceding book. What
is remarkable about *Men and Wives* is that the erstwhile victims,
without the slightest whimper, vigorously pursue the aims the
tyrant willed; but only after her death. Their change in attitude
exposes all the more prominently the point that it might not
have been of overwhelming importance whether Matthew married Camilla, whether Griselda married her rector, whether
Jermyn wrote poetry, or whether Gregory took tea with elderly
ladies: the important thing is that the individual does what he
does because *he wants* to do it. The fact that all the children
do at last undertake the aims set for them by Harriet after her
murder simply attests to their horror at the fact that *she* was
violently deprived of her will, however maniacally she prose-
cuted it when alive. That they followed her dictates does not
mean that she was right; it indicates that they regret the necessity for a calamity in order to establish their freedom of choice.

In addition, the mechanisms by which power ironically de-
feats itself within the family are given a classically definitive
treatment. Harriet works most easily with the weak-willed, obsequious Sir Godfrey whom she can manage almost as if he consti-
tuted a secondary extension of her own will. But when she is in
the mental institution, the same weakness leads Sir Godfrey to
squander money on every one of the indulgences that she has
held in check. While she is able to prevent his remarriage after
her death by the terms of an inflexible will, the weak minion
is really no lasting assurance to the tyrant that his will must
prevail. Jermyn and Griselda are intermediate figures who

perform the tyrant's commands when they must and who ignore them when they can. Gregory, the most abjectly devoted of her charges, is lashed to Harriet by bands of steel because of his peculiar penchant for elderly ladies; but this very advantage has its drawback in that he is necessarily devoted to *all* elderly ladies in the neighborhood, and, like most tyrants, Harriet demands exclusive attention. If none of these persons represents worthy adversaries, Matthew, who is most like his mother and can thus understand the full import of her wishes, knows that he must destroy her if he is to live at all.

In this novel, as in its predecessor, Miss Compton-Burnett handles with facility and grace a cast as large as an operatic chorus. In the minor characters, we have a typically broad range. Buttermere, the imperturbable butler, seems a first sketch for Bullivant of *Bullivant and the Lambs,* certainly one of the finest butlers in literature. In the same way, Sir Percy's second wife, Rachel Hardisty, who must live in the constant presence of the memories of his first wife, forecasts a generous handful of later characters. On the other hand, many of the types are already familiar. Lawyer Spong resembles Peter Bateman of *Brothers and Sisters* in his function as the unconsciously destructive gossip who transmits family secrets to the village; he differs from Peter in that his religious hypocrisy is fully exposed for what it is. Lady Haslam's grand tyranny is mirrored on a petty scale by Agatha Calkin, who bullies her two maiden sisters for their not having experienced the death of a spouse. She even aspires to challenging Harriet in her attempt to win over Gregory. Camilla Bellamy, one of two divorced women who appear in all the novels, wants "a lot of men and a lot of money and a lot of everything that can be touched and used." She is a rare "modern" type who intrudes on the village scene; the devastating skepticism of her conversation almost lends a Waugh touch. And her mother, addicted to worn literary clichés, is a Compton-Burnett figure who reappears frequently.

VI More Women than Men

In the first three mature novels, the final catastrophe (which, in the tradition of *Oedipus* and *Hippolytus,* may consist in the revelation of a truth as well as in an overt event) always occurred in the second or third from the last chapter, followed by a swift denouement. With *More Women than Men* (1933) the major catastrophe—Josephine Napier's killing her niece—occurs relatively early, in the fifteenth of twenty-four chapters. In this unusually long and leisurely denouement, at least one important revelation is given in Chapter XXII, but it hardly compares in importance with the dramatically represented murder.

In this novel the author returns to the school atmosphere of *Pastors and Masters* and to the ruthlessly possessive female tyrant. Josephine Napier, the owner of a girls' school, is determined to keep the affection of her nephew, Gabriel Swift, at any cost, including that of exposing his wife Ruth to a severe draft when the girl is at the height of a crisis in a severe case of pneumonia. This murder is echoed in an interlocking subplot of the "mirror" variety, since Ruth's mother, Elizabeth Giffard, had been in love with Josephine's husband Simon, but Josephine assured herself of Simon's attentions by petty lying. Now, after many years have elapsed, Elizabeth, weary and penniless, has thrown herself before Josephine, who hires her as a housekeeper. Josephine still hounds Elizabeth, and is in part responsible for Simon's death; for, when she surprises the pair in the library, Elizabeth involuntarily jerks back the ladder on which Simon is standing. He falls to his death.

Another interlocking subplot involves the intimate monosexual involvements that are an invariable element in Miss Compton-Burnett's school novels. Jonathan Swift, Josephine's brother, has for more than twenty years been the tutor and intimate companion of Felix Bacon, an irreverently Wildean aesthete whose actions and attitudes belie his forty years. On the distaff side, Maria Rosetti, one of the senior mistresses at Josephine's school, is widely known for her tender ministrations and close attachments to a succession of women. It is therefore an ironical revelation that Swift and Miss Rosetti, in a youthful indiscretion that they both regret, are the parents of Gabriel.

Because Maria accidentally witnessed Josephine's exposure of Ruth, she is bribed by the gift of a partnership in the school; but, when Josephine learns of Maria's youthful sin, the possibilities for blackmail are at an end. Josephine and Maria are both hard women; if there is any punishment in their having to live with each other, it is all they will receive.

In the school novel, the circle of village gossips is replaced by the school mistresses who chat in the common room. Since the mistresses are all unmarried or widowed females in a society that offers no other means of living, they are too dependent on Josephine to represent the relatively more independent force of the village gossips. As a result, Josephine's responsibility in the deaths of her husband and her niece is less generally known than would be similar acts in a "manor" novel. But without the automatic company of a dependent family, Josephine is also a lonelier figure than Sophia Stace or Harriet Haslam.

If many of the characters in this work are stock figures in the Compton-Burnett world, they do rise to scenes of individual assertion which make them memorable. Felix Bacon is outstanding among the subsidiary figures for an almost total reversal of character when he promises his dying father that he will marry and take over the estate. In the beginning of the novel he expressed mordant opposition to all claims of property, respectability, and convention; at the age of forty he is still literally nestling in the lap of his aged tutor. The crowning perversity of his lazy youth is his agreement to teach drawing in a girls' school, which prompts his gruff father to ask him if he will be required to wear petticoats. His absolute capitulation to the most pious reverence for the memory of his father constitutes one of Miss Compton-Burnett's wisest observations of a typical branch of human character.

In the family novels the innocent victims are granted a sharpness of repartee that compensates in its way for their hopeless dependence on the power figure. Elizabeth and Ruth Giffard, like the school mistresses, have been cowed by a hard life, and their complete dependence on Josephine's whim deprives them of the luxury of verbal retaliation. Even though the youth of the daughter and her relative independence as a married woman spur her to slightly more spirited opposition, both women remain mutely suffering figures with whatever nobility can be assigned to helplessness.

But the most memorable person remains Josephine Napier; the reader would have to go back to the Reverend Henry Bentley of *Pastors and Masters* to find a tyrant as unopposed as she. She manages her obsequious husband with the same ease that she displays in her relations with the hired help. Even Gabriel,

seemingly the only person to feel disinterested devotion for
his aunt, openly calls her an ogress; but he, too, submits to her
will. Her constant drive to turn the most naked self-seeking
into the appearance of concern for others is best seen in the deep
mourning she affects for a husband whose death hardly touches
her. In her library, she unashamedly dangles purse strings and
apron strings in the eyes of dependents, and then within a few
minutes she tells her docile audience in the common room of
her munificence. In fact, one of her most significant distinctions
is the whip-crack suddenness with which she can make hypocritical adjustments. A few hours after she has murdered Ruth,
she pretends elaborate regret at not having been nicer in petty
household matters; and she actually says that she would rather
have murdered Ruth than to have these memories on her con-
science. Ultimately, in her complete failure to command the
love of others, she is a somberly unhappy figure, too unhappy
even to know the degree of her depression.

Like Harriet's power, Josephine's is self-defeating. Once
she has disposed of Ruth Giffard in order to assure herself of
the undivided devotion of Gabriel, she slowly comes to the
realization that Felix Bacon has in the meantime supplanted
Gabriel in her affections. In her own officious way she decides
she will arrange for Gabriel's remarriage—to Helen Keats, the
teacher of classics. But even her powerful meddling cannot
nullify the sudden attraction of Felix to Miss Keats. There is
no possibility of returning to Gabriel, for he has gradually learned
of most of Josephine's unscrupulous ways, although he never
suspects her responsibility for Ruth's death. As Felix carries
Helen Keats off as a bride and as Gabriel decides to set up a
separate household for his father and Elizabeth Giffard, Josephine goes off to interview the new drawing mistress, a lonely,
bitter woman.

Part of Josephine's unhappiness can be attributed to a sexual
ambivalence much more complex than that of Jonathan Swift
or Maria Rosetti, who, if they are attracted to members of their
own sex, are at least attracted. There is in Josephine, by contrast,
a subtle but insistent hostility to sexual expression since it is
irrelevant to the major tensions of the power situations in which
she glories. She obviously married Simon merely to show that

she could steal him from Elizabeth, and her interest, as a middle-aged woman, in Felix and in Gabriel is largely for the pleasure of the exclusive, unremitting companionship which she means to extract. This hostility finds its most explicit expression in her nasty speeches just before the marriage of Gabriel and Ruth, speeches in which she accuses a placidly normal young couple of beastly lust.

VII   A House and Its Head

As if in reaction against the concentrated intensity of the school empire, Miss Compton-Burnett turned to a more complexly diffuse situation in her next novel, *A House and Its Head* (1935). What is lost in sharpness of focus is augmented by the laminated ironies of this complex household; of all the novels until this time, this one shows the richest fecundity of invention. To carry out this task, Miss Compton-Burnett puts a larger cast of characters through a series of intricate developments, including three marriages on the part of the *paterfamilias*.

After shortening the life of his first wife Ellen by forcing her to preside at meals despite a mortal illness, Duncan Edgeworth marries Alison, thirty-nine years younger than he. In the course of time, Alison produces a son, Richard, who is unmistakably fathered by Grant Edgeworth, Duncan's nephew, who is being groomed to take over the estate; the first irony, of course, is that Grant's illegitimate child will disinherit him. Second, Alison transfers her attentions from Grant to a neighborhood boy, Almeric Bode, who is also loved by Sibyl Edgeworth, Duncan's daughter and eventually Grant's wife. Sibyl, jealous of Alison's running off with Almeric, and bitter in the knowledge that Grant's illegitimate son by Alison will disinherit her own children, bribes a discharged nurse to turn on the gas in the nursery. Although Sibyl tries to transfer the guilt to Cassandra, the former governess and now Duncan's third wife, the family learns of her complicity in the matter; she is exiled for a short period but manages to gain a rich aunt's legacy, and the family then welcome her back with her newfound riches.

Duncan Edgeworth, the first of the line of Miss Compton-Burnett's male tyrants, employs many of the same tricks as his three immediate predecessors—Sophia Stace, Harriet Haslam,

and Josephine Napier. He is followed in this tradition by Horace
Lamb, Cassius Clare, Miles Mowbray, and Simon Challoner
of the later novels.

At the beginning and end of the Christmas which he has
ruined by his whining, avarice, temper, and self-assertion,
Duncan pointedly requires each member of the household to
answer an innocently platitudinous question about New Year's
resolutions or how they enjoyed the day. This insistence that
they pay lip service to the amenities in order to disguise his
own horrible responsibility for their unhappiness is an exquisitely
perfected Fascist technique.

The extreme contradictions in his nature are indicated by his
materially contributing to Ellen's death and then by forcing
each of his daughters to reassure him by the hour of his regard
and tenderness for Ellen. Although he had held Ellen to a
niggardly household budget that embarrassed her before the
servants, he proposes a lavishly expensive memorial in the
cemetery. His daughter Nance almost qualifies as an amateur
psychologist for the incisiveness with which she summarizes
these ill-sorted contradictions; she says that he manages to play
the roles of a sorrowing widower and a happy husband simul-
taneously, just as he is always as much the ruler as the martyr.

All the victims in earlier novels had been relatively blameless,
with the exception of Matthew Haslam, who was wildly goaded
to murder by Harriet. If anything extenuates Duncan's position,
it is that his minions Alison, Grant, and Sibyl prove themselves
capable of almost promiscuous illicit sexual passion and infanticide.

A more neutral figure, Oscar Jekyll, is a totally skeptical rector
who is constrained to continue in his ministry for purely
economic reasons; the next to last of the author's line of
churchmen who copiously filled the pages of *Dolores* and
Pastors and Masters, Oscar is the most sympathetic. In order
to protect her daughter Cassandra, his long-suffering and bitterly
wise mother Gretchen masterfully exposes how the murder of
baby Richard was managed.

Due to the seeming triumph of evil and evildoers in many
of these novels, the wholesomely good persons like Cassie (Cassandra) are often overlooked—not because they are unimportant,
but because they are overshadowed by the enormity of the

others. Like Patmore, the more than motherly sustainer of the Stace children, Cassie remains calm and strong in every crisis; her master, having harried one wife to her grave, and having driven a second to two adulterous unions, finally makes Cassie a legal mother to the children she educated. Her willingness to marry the tyrant without a demur is one of the most incisive demonstrations of Miss Compton-Burnett's levelheaded good sense. Cassie would be in an impossible position as a superannuated governess if she did not find a husband by the time the children were grown; she knows Duncan, and she has nursed his children through his most horrendous cruelties. The faint touch of resignation in her action goes along with the assurance that she is at least continuing in a familiar and predictable set of circumstances.

Alison, the unfortunate second wife, recalls Rachel Hardisty of *Men and Wives* in her uncomfortable domestic situation. Where Rachel is haunted by her predecessor's portrait in the dining room, Alison makes such a portrait an occasion for so much humor that her husband, who has moved it from the stairway in an access of hypocritical grief, restores it to the original place. Alison also has a faint resemblance to Camilla Bellamy, at least in the multiplicity of her lovers, but she lacks the former beauty's hard cynicism.

Lydia Fletcher of *Pastors and Masters,* with her works of charity and men's Bible classes, is an archetypal minor figure that blossoms into Beatrice Fellowes of *A House and Its Head,* the shyly bumptious religious type who goes from home to home on Christmas Day to reiterate to her largely unwilling audience "the simple message of Christmas." In her earnest do-good rivalry with her cousin Rosamund Burtenshaw, a retired missionary, she provides a comic element not unlike Emmeline Grangerford in *Huckleberry Finn.* A typical concern is which one can get into mourning first, after a neighborhood tragedy. Their friend Dulcia Bode, who makes the third disappointed rival for the rector's hand, is a lineal descendant of Tilly Bateman of *Brothers and Sisters,* although Dulcia has an edge on Tilly in intelligence, which she egregiously employs in her bustling, busybody interference with the affairs of others. As a trio, Beatrice, Rosamund, and Dulcia represent Miss Compton-Burnett's most devastating attack on all sanctimonious bustlers who know better than we what we are suffering, what will console us, and how many others ought to be made to share our intimate trials.

These novels do not occur, as some critics suggest, in a spatial and temporal vacuum. Even though Miss Compton-Burnett is not the kind of writer who catalogs realistic details, there are ample indications of the Victorian ambience. Duncan Edgeworth, for example, adds to the tensions of the Christmas breakfast scene at the opening of the novel by throwing into the fire an advanced scientific work which Grant has requested as a gift from Ellen. Like Henry James, who never reveals the product on which Mrs. Newsome's fortune is based in *The Ambassadors,* Miss Compton-Burnett does not name the text, any more than she reveals which biblical passage proves so embarrassing to Mrs. Merry in *Pastors and Masters* when her little pupils ask for a more literal rendering. But this very reticence about specific detail makes the suggestion that much more authentic since each reader can easily supply his own favorite Bible text.

The exquisite ironies of this narration nearly defy exegesis. Marshall, the nurse who is bribed to kill Grant's illegitimate child, was herself discharged because of Grant's attentions to her. The money used for the bribe comes from the sale of a diamond brooch that Sibyl received from Duncan when she married Grant. The murdered child would not only have disinherited Sibyl and Grant, but he is also a sign that Grant succumbed to Alison's charms before he married Sibyl, just as Alison also stole Almeric from Sibyl. With all this infighting within the same household, it is little wonder that when Grant, Sibyl, and her sister Nance are reunited in the schoolroom at the end of the novel, the conversation bristles with speeches of a black irony: the unspeakableness of the sentiments is equaled only by their universality in the human breast. Except for Cassie, nearly every major character has enough regrettable weaknesses to prevent him from sitting in judgment on anyone else. We can only repeat, with Emily Herrick, that good is bad condensed.

VIII *Conclusion*

In the first six novels, there is a steady growth in technical finesse. *Pastors and Masters* makes the first substantial claim on the conversational method, and it is almost as if the author were so preoccupied with what could be done in terms of characterization and the development of individual scenes that she ignored the plot almost entirely. The plot device of attempted plagiarism, when it comes to light in the penultimate chapter, is almost an afterthought. But with *Brothers and Sisters*, the sureness of Miss Compton-Burnett's achievement is absolute. Sixteen major characters move with ease through a steadily developed train of events in which they all function perfectly; the alternation of chapters, by which we catch glimpses of five different households and their contrasting reactions to the same events, demonstrates a masterful control of material.

Of the three novels involving murder, *More Women than Men* is the weakest as a total work; but some of its situations and characters are as impressive as anything in the author's *oeuvre*. *Men and Wives* is the closest of all Miss Compton-Burnett's works to a "modernist" anomaly—with the divorced rector, the interest in mental derangement, and the *nouveau-riche* milieu. But of all these works, *A House and Its Head* is the most complex, intricate, and tightly packed book, a fitting culmination to this period of the author's early high achievement.

In terms of plot development, *Pastors and Masters*, with its great crisis in the penultimate chapter, followed by a dinner that collects all the characters together in the last chapter, establishes a pattern that is very common in later novels, with the exception of *More Women than Men* in which the catastrophe occurs near the middle of the book. In addition, *Brothers and Sisters* and *A House and Its Head* are characterized by a series of lesser crises well spaced throughout the action.

Although *Brothers and Sisters* contains sparkling, witty comedy that is echoed by the scenes involving Felix Bacon in *More Women than Men*, the four novels that follow *Pastors and Masters* contain no fewer than eleven funerals which either occur or may be presumed to have occurred during the narration. Taken along with the murders, the incest, and the madness of Harriet Haslam, this may easily represent the most dour passage in the author's whole work, although none of her novels can be called sunny.

CHAPTER 3

A Beautiful Family Talk

"It will be a beautiful family talk, mean and
worried and full of sorrow and spite and
excitement."—*A Family and a Fortune*

I *Children and Servants*

THE next six novels continue many of the distinctive Compton-Burnett characteristics with which we are familiar; the
most striking new feature of this period is the preoccupation with
childhood experience that runs through *Daughters and Sons*
(1937), *Parents and Children* (1941), *Elders and Betters* (1944),
Bullivant and the Lambs (1947), and *Two Worlds and Their
Ways* (1949). Only *A Family and a Fortune* (1939) ignores
the very young. There is also in this period an increase in what
we might call the "diptych" or balanced novel in which children are posed against adults, school against manor milieu, or
servants against masters. Particularly in *Elders and Betters* and
in *Bullivant and the Lambs* do the servants take a prominent role,
the butler of the latter volume asserting himself as one of the
finest character creations in all the Compton-Burnett works.

II Daughters and Sons

As if the author had made a final consolidation of technique
in the earlier works, she introduces several new features in
Daughters and Sons (1937). In the first place, we have two
masterful and scheming tyrants in the same house, the elderly
Sabine Ponsonby and her maiden daughter Henrietta. These two
have reached a kind of *façon de vivre* by staking out separate
empires. Hetta (Henrietta) directs the parsimonious economy of
the household and entirely dominates the work of her brother
John, a hard-working and successful novelist. Sabine supervises

the education and manners of John's five children, since their mother is dead.

Second, in this range of characters, Sabine, who is eighty-four, and her granddaughter Muriel Ponsonby, who is eleven, represent new extremes of characterization in age and youth; and, for first efforts in this direction, both remain memorable portraits of types that the author comes to employ with increasing frequency. Sabine's wearily irritable senility is countered by Muriel's constant giggling at the eating habits of her governess. Muriel is just on the verge of entering the social world. She appears at dinner only on the hiring of a new governess—which is a frequent occurrence in this tightly reined matriarchy—but these occasions provide a richly comic opportunity.

Third, in *Daughters and Sons* the author makes full-fledged use of the "false scent" in plot development, which was initiated by Harriet Haslam's suicide attempt in *Men and Wives*. The first instance is Hetta's farewell note, written after her brother John has remarried, which suggests she has committed suicide. Although she hopes to prove to the family the indispensability of her services, she actually demonstrates that the house can be managed very well without her. The second false scent is the village rumor that Sabine disinherited her family in favor of the tutor Alfred. When he firmly announces to the family that he will return only one half of the legacy to them, he unnecessarily reveals his meanness of spirit, for the actual will has no provision for his inheriting the estate.

Finally, Miss Compton-Burnett dispenses with the prying gossip as a primary means of transmitting family doings to the village. Toward the end of the novel, in a fantastically condensed speech to a dinner table of local residents, Hetta herself hysterically spills out the whole train of events that culminates in her deposition from authority. At the same time, the shock of the speech itself, and of what it reveals, results in the death of Sabine right at the table. Here, indeed, a speech becomes a death-dealing event in its own right, as is only fitting in a dialogue novel.

In brief, John's daughter France won a literary prize, but had submitted her book in the name of the governess, Edith Hallam, since she feared her novelist father's jealousy. This substitution of names led Sabine to think the governess a rich woman, so she secretly persuaded John to marry Edith for her money. As Hetta says in her grand speech, after reviewing these events: "'What a welter of deceit I have found in my family! What a moral mess I have stumbled on unawares, stumbled on because it was everywhere. First Mater must deceive us all; then she deceived you; then you deceived Edith. Now Edith has begun to deceive you, though I admit she was afraid. France had already deceived you, though I admit she was afraid'" (280-81).

In contrast to the relative diffusion of event in *A House and Its Head*, the plot of *Daughters and Sons* returns to the simple, more tightly screwed construction of the earlier novels. Divided into twelve fairly long chapters, the book rises to the climax of Hetta's false suicide in Chapter X and then in Chapter XI to her catastrophic revelation of family deceit which kills Sabine. In addition, there is a regular counterpoint of symmetrical repetitions in plot situations that ties together a series of subsidiary situations. For example, in Chapter III Sabine comes to Miss Marcon's home to interview her nephew, Alfred, for the position of tutor. Although she is accompanied by two grandchildren, Clare and Chilton, she requires them to wait out of sight since she does not wish to strain the hospitality of Miss Marcon's cottage. Her little social ruse is exposed by the rain, which drives Clare and Chilton indoors. In Chapter VIII Miss Marcon has come to the Ponsonby home to ferret out the gossip about John's coming marriage, and she encounters Sir Rowland and his son Evelyn Seymour near the entrance, bent on the same mission. She persuades them, too, to stand out of sight while she enters the house; they, too, are caught and exposed by the rain.

Dr. Chaucer, the fat and foolish rector, seems fated to imbroglios with Ponsonby governesses. When his niece, Miss Bunyan, leaves the position, she comes to keep house for him. He proposes to the next governess, Miss Hallam, and is rejected just as summarily as he is by the succeeding governess, Miss Blake, who leaves her position since she assumes he has insulted her. When he finally settles on Hetta as the best of a bad bargain, the circle is completed by Miss Bunyan's return to the Ponsonby house.

Alfred's false airs of grandeur when he thinks he has been

willed Sabine Ponsonby's fortune are an echo of the proud but mistaken pleasure John Ponsonby takes in Chapter VI when he receives a check from an anonymous reader. He announces to a grand dinner party—the same guests attend the dinner when Hetta makes her revelation—that the check is in payment for a debt of gratitude that all readers owe to great writers. And his discomfiture is as great as Alfred's when he discovers that the check was in reality sent by his daughter France in an attempt to tide him over household debts without arousing his jealousy because his daughter is a better writer than he.

In Chapter V Hetta testily upbraids the new governess for missing morning prayers and their sustaining benefits; when Hetta disappears in Chapter XI, we learn that the young people are slow to miss her because she seldom appears at morning prayers herself.

For an author who works with the virtuosity of Miss Compton-Burnett, it is difficult to make relative judgments, but *Daughters* probably excels many of her other novels in the brilliance of the rapid-fire repartee between the armed camps of the bullies and the bullied. The insistent whispered wit of the young people goads Sabine to the extent that, in a gesture of frustration, she accidentally strikes her grandson Victor with her cane. In Chapter VIII there is a maddeningly funny byplay on Muriel's stolid silence when she is asked to address the new governess, only to be followed by ingenuously naïve questions when she does talk.

The other grandchildren exasperate Sabine into demanding silence "almost on a shriek," before their barbed chatter drives her from the room. But the most glittering pyrotechnical display of the book is in the conversation preceding Hetta's set address in Chapter XI; not only does the family indulge in disastrously frank badinage, but the guests, too, provide a fugal accompaniment in their barely audible comments.

III   A Family and a Fortune

Neither the tyrant nor the fortune of *A Family and a Fortune* (1939), Miss Compton-Burnett's eighth novel, is in the immediate family. By a symmetry already familiar in her works, the tyrant, Matty, is a maiden sister of the *materfamilias* and the fortune comes to Dudley, a bachelor brother of the *paterfamilias*.

One of her nephews remarks of the indomitable Matty Seaton,
" 'She is at once super and subhuman. I always wonder if she
is a goddess or a beast' " (65). She is an ogre of self-regard;
as a partial invalid she savagely overworks and browbeats the
poor Miss Griffin who has given her life as a paid companion.
By contrast, Dudley Gaveston, the bachelor brother, is a figure
of quiet charm and wit, a favorite of the children. He is largely
distinguished by his contentment at giving all he can for the
happiness of others.

When Dudley comes into a fortune, he distributes it with
accustomed bountifulness; but it eventually undermines his
habit of renunciation. He announces he will withdraw his many
grants in order to marry Maria Sloane, an old friend of Matty's.
But before the marriage can occur, Blanche Gaveston, the *materfamilias*, dies. During Dudley's absence on a business trip necessitated by the death, Edgar, Dudley's brother, wins the affection of Maria. Dudley is greeted on his return by the announced engagement. In the ensuing argument, he quits his
brother's roof at about the same time that Matty, in one of her
fits of ungovernable temper, drives Miss Griffin out into the
snow; the two fugitives meet *en route*, and in finding succor
for Miss Griffin, Dudley contracts a serious illness himself. Miss
Griffin nurses him back to his former gentle state.

When the whole family settles back into the manor on a new
basis born of these complex insights, and as Dudley announces
he will restore all the allowances, the young people discuss their
emotional reaction to the situation. In this dialogue, Miss
Compton-Burnett makes a clear and open acknowledgment of
the sort of mixed form she is working in. Justine Gaveston, the
eldest daughter of Edgar and Blanche, remarks to her brothers
Clement and Aubrey:

". . . It was a great failure. Surely one of those that are greater
than success."

"I never quite know what those are. I suppose you mean other
kinds of success. The same kind involves the same effort and has
a better end."

"And a much more convenient one," said Clement.

"Yes, yes, more convenient," said Justine. "But what we have seen
was surely something more than that."

"Something quite different indeed," said Mark.

"Surely it was worth it."

"From our point of view as spectators?"

"Well, in the sense that all human effort must achieve something essential, even if not apparent!" (260)

This discussion is obviously something like the essential core of tragedy: the failure that must, by some paradoxical meaning, be counted a success. Justine has just remarked, in fact, that the experience has "transfigured" her. But in the very next speech Aubrey, by dwelling on the ludicrous picture of Miss Griffin and Uncle Dudley in the snow, reduces the group to laughter. He returns to the same subject a bit later:

"Miss Griffin and Uncle walking through the snow, with Miss Griffin wearing Uncle's coat and hat!" murmured Aubrey.

"She was not wearing his hat. She—she"—said Justine, going into further laughter—"had a shawl round her head. Oh, why are we laughing? Why cannot we take a serious view of what is serious and even tragic in itself? Miss Griffin's long relation with Aunt Matty broken? Because I suppose it is the break. And her life at sixes and sevens, because that must be the truth. And we cannot see it without being diverted by silly, little, surface things which in themselves have their tragic side, just because they touch our superficial sense of humour." Justine's voice quavered away as this again happened to her. "I suppose we are half hysterical; that is what it is."

"That is the usual explanation of unseemly mirth," said Mark. (260-61)

But this hysteria is not in itself a sufficient answer. The true reason for the mixed reaction of transfiguration and laughter lies in the significant reference in the preceding quotation to the young people's considering the whole matter from a spectator's point of view. Their immediate fate will be decided by the action, but they are not themselves protagonists; and it is this very distance that puts into disproportion the "silly, little, surface things" and destroys the heroic frame of reference essential to classical tragedy. What we have is a tragic situation refracted through the prism of comedy of manners.

When Dudley leaves the Gaveston roof, his measured and stately speech to his brother and sister-in-law, Edgar and

Blanche, whose home he has shared, is a half-philippic, half-tragic renunciation:

"You have lost your brother! Then know that you have lost him. Know that you speak the truth. You may be glad to be left with your wife, and I shall be glad to leave you. I shall be glad, Edgar. I have always been alone in your house, always in my heart. You had nothing to give. You have nothing. There is nothing in your nature. You did not care for Blanche. You do not care for your children. You have not cared for me. You have not even cared for yourself, and that has blinded us. May Maria deal with you as you are, and not as I have done." (234-35)

When such a man returns to the home where he has uttered this speech and is seen in the final tableau walking arm in arm with Edgar, some kind of hysteria is needed to relieve the situation.

The intermingling of good and evil is especially pointed in the last chapter, when it is accidentally discovered that Clement Gaveston is a miser who has hoarded gold coins in his bedroom. Dudley remarks that it was bad enough he went into a jealous rage and that Matty drove Miss Griffin out into the cold night, but Clement's miserliness now proves that they all have their ridiculous moments.

Matty is very slightly distinguished from earlier tyrants in that she exercises her doleful power from a cottage on the estate, rather than from inside the manor as in the preceding cases; coupled with her invalidism, this removal from the scene ought to shackle her. But in the speed and certainty with which she appears at the manor just in time for each crisis—despite even snow in one case—one suspects that a certain amount of her lameness is dissembled. She manages to attain a degree of fiendishness that is at least as intense as that of the best of the tyrants. In the long-suffering Miss Griffin, she has an ideally helpless victim on whom to inflict all the screaming rage and cruelty that well up from her own lonely and loveless soul. Her second victim—and her access to a whole family of minions—is her meek sister Blanche who only reveals her reaction to this lifelong browbeating on her deathbed; in a final delirium Blanche asserts that her own mind and heart are at least slightly superior to Matty's.

Blanche's daughter Justine, the oldest of the children and the only girl, is as complex as any woman in Compton-Burnett novels. Her position in the family has made her an officious and bumptious woman whose limited intelligence leads her to make several very serious, if well-intentioned, errors of judgment that have the worst consequences for the family. For example, it is Justine who throws Edgar and Maria together during the absence of Dudley. To the systematic reader, Justine's resemblance to Tilly Bateman of *Brothers and Sisters* and to the triad of pushy busybodies of *A House and Its Head* immediately classifies her as a standard minor comic character. But this is a misleading resemblance because—although Justine has all of their speed in unleashing clichés, in assuming that she knows the feelings of others better than they do, and in masking her own self-satisfaction behind the standard Christian virtues—these very failings turn out to be advantages. It takes someone as self-assured and as obtuse as Justine to stand up to Matty and to precipitate the family rebellion that almost literally drives Matty from the house just before she retaliates by driving Miss Griffin out into the snow. In regretting this snap judgment about Justine, the reader is also prompted to see Tilly, Dulcia, Beatrice, and Rosamund in a new light; and he is certainly impelled to marvel again at the breadth and elevation of the author's moral sympathies.

In structure, this novel resembles *Brothers and Sisters* and *Daughters and Sons* in a ten-to-twelve-chapter length with the major catastrophe occurring two or three chapters from the end. Its tightness is augmented by the absence of villagers, aside from Mr. and Mrs. Middleton and the very sketchily presented Dr. Marlowe.

IV Parents and Children

Dudley Gaveston's feeling that Matty's cruelty and Clement's avarice mitigate his own jealousy is echoed in the next novel, *Parents and Children* (1941). Here, too, the sins of one camp are held out by the characters as extenuations for sins in the other. The book also has the twelve-chapter compactness, with a resounding climax in the eleventh chapter that makes up in excitement what it lacks in plausibility.

Fulbert Sullivan, required to spend six months in South

America, writes that he is mortally ill and may be presumed dead if a cable is not received before his letter. His wife Eleanor shortly afterward decides to marry Ridley Cramner, the man her husband has appointed to take care of his affairs. On the day before the wedding, Fulbert returns, and it is dramatically revealed that Ridley was aware of his existence but had hoped to postpone general knowledge of this fact until after Eleanor's bigamous union with him. In retaliation at his own exposure, Ridley reveals that Sir Jesse, Fulbert's father, on his own youthful trip to South America, fathered the three Marlowe orphans who live in a lodge on the estate. " 'If you judge me, so do I judge you,' said Ridley to Sir Jesse. 'And I say you are worse than I' " (268).

Aside from these resemblances to its predecessors in the balancing off of moral failures, *Parents and Children* reveals a number of very subtle differences from earlier novels. The tyrant figure, Eleanor Sullivan, shows few of the pyrotechnics that distinguish her avatars; a woman of narrow sympathies and shallow intelligence, she hardly has the imagination for evil on a grand scale. Her unwilling dependence on her in-laws seriously hampers her position, and the nine brilliantly witty and sensitive children, ranging in age from three to twenty-four, are quite beyond her control. Their conventional manners barely disguise their hostility and revulsion for her. If she had had the wits to realize her good fortune, she might have been more grateful to her husband's parents, the volcanic Sir Jesse and the dourly possessive Regan, for their inhibitive effect on her offspring.

Of greater importance in terms of the author's whole development as a novelist is the range of childhood portraits, by far the most ambitious that Miss Compton-Burnett had attempted in her novels to this point. Luce represents the typically good but talkative elder daughter, and Daniel and Graham are the standard collegiate types who carry on a steady war of nerves with their barely audible cynicisms. Of the schoolroom contingent, the delicate Isabel and her attractive sister Venetia are deeply loyal to their father, but James is isolated by his especially difficult transitional age. In the nursery, Honor and Gavin form a vigorous pair of intimates, set off by the egocentrism of the three-year-old Nevill, a brilliant confirmation of the promises inherent in Muriel Ponsonby of *Daughters and Sons*.

While all of the children are remarkably individualized, Nevill Sullivan stands out in the reader's memory. Miss Compton-Burnett gains some of her most brilliant comic effects from her sure sense of the mental age of each of the children and of the reactions typical of that level to various experiences. Nevill has not yet learned to distinguish between personal pronouns, so that his third-person statements about himself carry a ludicrously formal air. He has a tenacious memory for rote learning, as is seen in his unerring association of certain colors with certain letters as he learns his alphabet. But this same faculty has disastrous results as he repeats to his returned father the rote phrases taught him as consolation for that father's supposed death and for the mother's substitution of a new father for her children. And he plays a relatively important role in the plot, for it is his exploration of Ridley's pockets that leads to the latter's exposure.

The relative simplicity and implausibility of the "Enoch Arden" plot has rich compensation in the increase of patterned symmetry in this novel. There are repeated tours of the schoolroom and the nursery by Eleanor herself, by the Cramner family, by Eleanor and her prospective husband Ridley, and finally by Eleanor and her restored husband Fulbert. Happily, the visitors are nearly always discomfited in their attempts to foist some uncongenial attitude on the children. The tenderhearted Faith Cramner tries to dissuade the children from making bows and arrows to shoot innocent birds, but, before they have finished with her, she might well wish that she had ignored the subject entirely.

This same state of affairs assumes greater importance when Eleanor tries to require poignant regret at her remarriage of the children at the same time that she wants them to feel happiness at her improved state. But the children are far too wise to be long perplexed by this contradiction; in their conversational gambits they explore the embarrassing complexities of remarriage. Why can't mother go on having children if Queen Anne had eighteen? Does mother know that she is renouncing all hope of being received by Queen Victoria? Does she love Ridley more than she did Fulbert?

Another very complex set of repetitions centers about a series
of photographs that reveal Sir Jesse's early peccadilloes.

Ranged against the children are a full battery of nurses, maids,
and governesses—Emma Hatton, Bertha Mullet, Miss Mitford,
and Miss Pilbeam. Like Patmore of *Brothers and Sisters,* Hatton
is an *ersatz* mother, but she is infinitely more consoling to the
younger children than their real mother. Mullet, her subordinate,
provides a charming foil to the events of the plot in her exaggerated tales of her own family life, which the children themselves (who are wiser than some of Miss Compton-Burnett's
critics) come to realize are patent lies; she simply embroiders
on recent events in the Sullivan household, always pitching them
one key lower in tragedy, despair, or meanness. Unlike many
a Compton-Burnett governess, Miss Mitford is secretly quite
happy, and she has the good sense not to reveal this either to
her charges or to her employer. Her steady good spirits are based
on omnivorous reading and the eating of chocolates. Again
unlike the governesses of *Daughters and Sons,* Miss Pilbeam
is not at all suited by education for her position—except in the
classical tricks of her profession for keeping a half-step ahead of
her pupils. She is successful in all departments but doing sums,
where Honor palpably shames her to her face.

Miss Pilbeam's plight, as the unmarried daughter of a vet-
erinarian who has a very small income, is echoed by the dilemma
of the Marlowes. Sir Jesse grants his three illegitimate children
just enough to meet the necessities of life. The income from
Susan's position as a teacher and from Lester's books is not
even enough to provide them with firewood, but their gentility
forces them to wait until nightfall to go about the estate collecting fallen beechwood. Even in the manor, penury haunts
the minds of the dependent children. They are incessantly reminded of Sir Jesse's bounty and of the excessive cost of their
education, but they are equally upbraided for the natural consequence of joking references to workhouses and paupers'
graves.

In *Parents and Children,* as in its two predecessors—*Daughters
and Sons* and *A Family and a Fortune*—there is no crime to
equal those of the novels treated in the preceding chapter. Sir
Jesse's youthful wild oats are held up against Ridley's attempt
to force Eleanor into a bigamous union. Eleanor's own speed in

deciding to remarry is not held against her by her husband, either. Because these are all lapses of passion or weakness rather than positive crimes, it is the emotional tensions and irritations of the children that prove the most painful element in the novel. Bewildered and frustrated by Eleanor's selfish hypocrisy and by their father's distraction and absence, their suffering makes the novel a kind of domestic elegy. The losses of the children are not catastrophic, but their spiritual loneliness is consistently saddening.

V Elders and Betters

Miss Compton-Burnett and her friend Margaret Jourdain fled London during the bombings of World War II, and it is perhaps this interruption of domestic habit that accounts for the delay in the appearance of *Elders and Betters* (1944), which is one of the few breaks in the author's consistent writing schedule.

The title, which could only be taken ironically, indicates Miss Compton-Burnett's continuing concern with childhood experience, although Dora and Julius Calderon, the ten- and eleven-year-olds of this novel, do not have quite the prominence of Nevill Sullivan or of Muriel Ponsonby. When we first encounter them, however, we realize that they differ from many of the author's other children characters in the fiendish way that they calculatingly use childlike traits for their own advantage, out of a wisdom far more seasoned and balanced than that of any of the bumbling adults.[1] We first come upon them on their knees in the garden, praying to their own personal god who inhabits a particular rock. They have clearly invented their *ersatz* religion because they are conscious of their difference from the adults about them, and yet they always leave the door open a crack for a retreat to the established faith.

When their father Thomas decides, after the suicide of his wife Jessica, to marry a girl forty-two years younger than he, he earnestly asks them to accept her as a new mother. When she finally decides against the marriage, Thomas asks Dora and Julius to keep the memory of their mother sacred. These demands are similar to those required of the Sullivan children, and the Calderons react in the same way by showing up their parents' hypocrisy in simple, direct questions. As Julius devastatingly remarks, in another context, " 'Children should not

IVY COMPTON-BURNETT

be used for the outlet of grown-up people's guilty feelings. What have we to do with their remorse? It is the due reward of their deeds'" (113). Our last view of these precocious children is again at the rock in the garden as they pray for strength to sustain the childish pose that their father requires of them.

At the level of the adult characters, many of the plot situations of *Elders and Betters* echo those of earlier novels. We have the Calderon family in the manor house, with the poorer Donne relations in a nearby cottage—like the Langs in *Brothers and Sisters,* the Seatons in *A Family and a Fortune,* and the Marlowes in *Parents and Children.* As in *Daughters and Sons,* there are two major tyrants in the *Elders,* the invalid Susan (Sukey) Donne in the manor, and her niece Anna Donne in the cottage. Moreover, much of the plot centers around a will locked in a desk, like the letter of *Brothers and Sisters.*

But there are also sufficient distinctions. As an invalid tyrant, Sukey would resemble Matty Seaton, except that she has no faithful companion on whom to vent her rages; and Sukey is far more beautiful than Matty, which lends a streak of vanity to her other distasteful qualities. Under the constant fear of a heart attack, she repeatedly reminds her sister, brother, brother-in-law, nieces, nephews, and friends that each moment may be her last. But as her brother-in-law warns her, she not only cries "wolf" once too often but tires everyone in earshot by her selfish whining. Just at the point where Miss Compton-Burnett has the reader in the same mood, Sukey dies.

She has asked Anna to destroy a late will, made out in a fit of pique, which grants her fortune to Anna, and to preserve an earlier will which benefits the entire family. Anna does just the opposite so that she can afford to marry her cousin Terence Calderon, a butterfly type who resembles Felix Bacon of *More Women than Men* and Julian Wake of *Brothers and Sisters* in his brilliantly caustic perversity.

When Jessica, Sukey's sister, quietly pursues Anna with questions about the will, Anna retaliates by playing on Jessica's distraught nerves. She implies that Jessica is a hated, Satanic ogre, when her character is literally the opposite of that. Anna is so skillful in implying that Jessica is poisoning her own children's lives by her "'sinister, creeping force,'" that Jessica

[70]

commits suicide in the very room and chair in which Sukey died, using Sukey's medicines. Her daughter Tullia discovers the body, as she did Sukey's.

This novel, more than its predecessors, drew comment from critics about the seeming crassness of Anna's triumphant success in gaining the money and the mate she wanted by disregarding all human decency. It is partly with this novel in mind that Pamela Hansford Johnson referred to Ivy Compton-Burnett as "the most amoral of living writers."[2] This may do as a surface judgment since, as Miss Hansford Johnson points out, no other writer in the history of the novel has administered such moral shocks to his readers. But, on a second look, "amoral" implies a lack of moral standards, whereas Miss Compton-Burnett is obviously clear in her mind that there are very firm moral distinctions and that Anna Donne has torn them to unrecognizable shreds. The implication is that these standards were invented by human beings; and, like all standards set up by the decent majority, they are easily ignored by an unscrupulous individual overcome by greed and by sexual passion. As Ivy Compton-Burnett says in one of her interviews, there are signs that strange things happen in the privacy of family life and that they do not always come to public knowledge. One has only to look at statistics of a leading medical society about the number of infant deaths in which the body shows signs of sustaining severe bruises. The idea is abhorrent to a civilized society, but the statistics are there.

Chapter VI contains a memorable dinner scene which is a delight in itself, regardless of its function in the book as a whole. As the diners are about to seat themselves, someone remarks that they are a party of thirteen; Tullia adds that the first to sit will die within a specified period. As they all hesitate, the author manages to reveal subtle laminations of character in the various reactions to superstition, fear of death, courage, chivalry, and rank. The nearly unbearable tension is broken by Thomas's asserting that it is the last to sit who is doomed. In the flurry to sit down, Jessica—who does die shortly afterward by her own hand—is the last to do so. In a sense, the scene is emblematic of many of the features of Miss Compton-Burnett's art. In terms of real life, it is impossible to imagine the group as standing as long as it does, or as speaking with such controlled brilliance and variety; but for the reader who values aesthetic perfection above *vraisemblance*, the occasion is one of pure delight.

Cook and Ethel, the cottage contingent of servants, come as close to low comedy relief as any characters in the novels, although even here the crystalline purity of Miss Compton-Burnett's objectivity does not permit a condescending approach. Cook, squat and broad and dull, is mothered by the maid, who is tall and bright. For every one of Anna's sneers at the servants' superstitions or requests for better conditions, there are abundant gossip sessions with the eldest son Bernard, and placating gestures from Miss Jennings, the housekeeper. These servants seem to take on a nearly superhuman aspect in their infallible omniscience about events affecting the family. Not only do they know of events before most of the family, but one almost expects them to read the future.

The sons Bernard and Esmond are a rung lower than the typical gentry since they have followed in the path of their retired father—having government jobs in London. In his sympathy for the servants and even for Aunt Sukey, Bernard shows a larger nature than is usually encountered in Compton-Burnett sons. But Esmond's corrosively destructive and laconic remarks make up for Bernard's sympathies in full measure. The lame Reuben is a pathetic figure who is too young for his brothers and too old to play with Julius and Dora, who grant him only a subsidiary status in their garden rituals.

After the death of Jessica, *Elders* closes with a flurry of marriages unequaled since the denouement of *Brothers and Sisters*. Of the three engagements, two are between first cousins; as Anna remarks, " 'We shall be simmering in a family cauldron indeed' " (222).

VI   Bullivant and the Lambs

Miss Compton-Burnett's first postwar novel, *Manservant and Maidservant* (1947), attained popularity in America under the title *Bullivant and the Lambs* (1948). Although her admirers find it impossible to name any one book as their favorite since the consistency of quality is so high, many nevertheless think of *Bullivant* as one of her most memorable volumes. It is a narrative of compelling interest in which excitement carries the reader along at a familiar pace: curiosity tugs at his attention to read faster in order to discover the outcome, but the august nobility of the speeches makes him pause to savor the simple profundity of the style.

This book is unique in many of its features, and yet the very difference from earlier novels only underscores the abiding truths with which Miss Compton-Burnett habitually concerns herself. Most importantly, the tyrant Horace Lamb is the first one in these novels to see the error of his cruel and arbitrary power and to attempt to reform himself. During his wife Charlotte's absence on a long voyage, Horace stumbles upon a letter (artfully placed in his way by a lady enamored of his cousin Mortimer) which reveals that Charlotte and Mortimer mean to go off together with the children on her return. As a result of this forewarning, Charlotte is greeted by a reformed husband.

Chapter VI, which contains Charlotte's first encounter with the "new" Horace, presents a series of speeches of a noble grandeur that outstrip any other contemporary writing for plainspoken, earnest directness, coupled with the beauty of simplicity. Here, in one short sample, is Charlotte's address to Horace about their situation:

"You know that seeing her children suffer day by day will make any woman hard. You are not without ordinary knowledge. You are not so much a person apart. If you did not know such things, you would not have done as you have done. And you know the truth that lies behind us. You crushed the spring of childhood, bound it with constraint and fear, forced it to deception and visited the wrong you caused. You burdened and wrung a mother's heart. You did it month after month and year after year. You knew you were doing it. You know now what you did. Your present course proves your knowledge. I may speak well. I have often heard these words echoing in my heart, and wondered you did not hear them. I am saying them now, not to accuse you or spoil your efforts, but to vindicate the innocent. Mortimer and I did right, not wrong, as you did always wrong and never right. And now it is clear between us, and need not be said again."[3]

This interview is succeeded by one between Horace and Mortimer, which recalls that between Edgar and Dudley Gaveston in *A Family and a Fortune*. Horace commands his cousin to leave his house as soon as he can conveniently marry Magdalen Doubleday, the lady who dropped Charlotte's letter in Horace's way.

In Horace's wavering and backsliding efforts at reform, the effects of his domination on his children are infinitely more excruciating than they would be with a consistently overbearing parent. Once the children have been released from the grinding penury that does not permit fires in the winter and that forces the boys to wear their sisters' wornout dressing gowns, their blossoming of spirit is honest and straightforward. But when there is a threat of return to the *ancien régime*, the panic of the children is painful to observe. It reaches such proportions that Horace's own sons, Jasper and Marcus, find themselves powerless to warn him of a weakened bridge which is in his path. After he narrowly escapes from this danger, the interview with Jasper and Marcus elicits this moving response from the latter:

"We are afraid of you. You know we are. . . . Your being different for a little while has not altered all that went before. Nothing can alter it. You did not let us have anything; you would not let us be ourselves. If it had not been for Mother, we would rather have been dead. It was feeling like that so often, that made us think dying an ordinary thing. We had often wished to die ourselves. It is not the same with you as with other people. If anyone else did something, we should just see that thing. If you do it, it adds itself to all the rest. We cannot help it. Neither can you help it now. It is something that cannot be changed." (227)

The stark fatalism of this view is all the more affecting because it is the insight of a child.

The second great innovation in *Bullivant* is that at least half of the novel is devoted to the life of the servants below-stairs, with the dignified Bullivant, the finest of Miss Compton-Burnett's butlers, and the hymn-singing Mrs. Selden as rulers in their own right. They struggle soulfully to train the fat and simple orphan Miriam and the obstreperous workhouse boy George to a semblance of respect for their superiors. The servants' sure integration into the plot shows a great advance over the treatment of Cook and Ethel in *Elders and Betters*. At the same time, the servants' gossip replaces the earlier village busybodies of the manor novels and the school mistresses of the school novels.

When George is caught stealing a large supply of provisions in order to feast his village friends on his day off, he decides to commit suicide; but when he arrives at the gorge, he removes the danger sign from the same bridge that Horace nearly crossed earlier, depositing a knife he stole from Marcus near the scene. Horace, on another walk, nearly crosses the weakened bridge a second time; since he finds Marcus's knife on the scene, he assumes his sons have again attempted to allow him to die accidentally. On his return, he begins an even more excruciating scene with his sons than the earlier one, relieved only by the arrival of the tutor, Gideon Doubleday, who has seen George brandishing the same knife in the village store earlier in the afternoon.

Thus George's actual attempt on Horace's life parallels in a kind of grisly comic tone the failure of the boys to warn their father of the bridge in an earlier chapter. This is but one of a series of symmetrical correspondences between the family and the servants which hold the book together tightly.

Bullivant, who is Horace Lamb's counterpart below-stairs, is distinguished by a particularly strange physiognomy—one unusual in these novels except for that granted to Cook in *Elders and Betters.* Just as some of these plots might seem to be burlesques of Victorian melodramas, so one almost suspects Miss Compton-Burnett of satirizing the standard literary butler. Bullivant is punctilious, omniscient, superefficient, and absolutely unruffled by the most horrendous crises. His elaborate circumlocutions argue a verbal skill far beyond that of his employers. He has many of the qualities of Buttermere in *Men and Wives* and of Jellamy in *A Family and a Fortune,* but his great distinction from Buttermere is his inflexible loyalty to the family, which leads him to justify any avarice of Horace's, no matter how extreme. Bullivant knows he is dealing with the genuine thing, whereas Buttermere found himself in unwilling servitude to the *nouveau riche.* In Bullivant's patient explanations to George of the workings of hierarchy from royalty on down, from moment to moment one expects him to invoke Ulysses' speech from *Troilus,* so certain is his command of degree. On the other hand, it does not do to overlook George in any discussion of Bullivant, for he is the maddening exception that proves Bullivant's rules. A workhouse boy who sees no limit to the heights he may attain, and no call on himself to develop any faculties to be worthy of the ascent, he was placed on earth expressly to bedevil the Bullivants. Cook is primarily distinguished by her nonconformist faith, but curiously enough her antipathy to established ritual is accepted by Bullivant as a matter of course.

Horace's final bout with death is an attack of pneumonia, attendant on a new economy drive like that at the beginning of the novel in which he put the children through a program of calisthenics in the nursery to save coal. In the conviction that he will die shortly, Horace calls each of the children to his bedside and confesses his shortcomings in dealing with them: " 'My children, I bequeath to you the freedom and joy of life. If they depend on my leaving you, take them as your gift from me. I go willingly to give them to you. I mistrust myself, as you mistrust me!' " (279-80)

The horror of anyone's wishing to make, and of anyone else's having to receive, such a legacy is hardly mitigated by Horace's recovery. One wonders that his convalescence is not complicated by the knowledge that he must now live with the family whom he addressed thus. We can be certain that he deserves to have to live with the knowledge, and to that degree his recovery is a comic retribution. But the children remain, too. Thus the comedy, as always in a Compton-Burnett ending, has its somber colors.

VII   Two Worlds and Their Ways

If readers have been fond of *Bullivant and the Lambs*, the author herself has a marked preference for her next novel. She has said, "I think 'Two Worlds and Their Ways' [1949] one of my best books."[4] It is like *Bullivant and the Lambs* in that it is stitched together by a series of intricate parallels between the manor house and the schoolroom. The schoolroom takes the place of the kitchen in the former novel. These parallels are managed by one of Miss Compton-Burnett's most intricate and incredible plots, involving a pair of earrings that show up so often that one character remarks they might actually be reproducing young. Some critics have found these qualities in the plot a fault; but, aside from the author's own feeling about the book, we also have a refutation of these criticisms in the book itself. When the whole plot has been revealed near the end, this conversation appears:

"It is a trivial sort of a tale," said Mr. Firebrace.
"What a shallow word!" said his grandson. "When the facts are trivial, and it is itself rooted in the depths. It is the sort of thing that is a test, and you have failed."[5]

This may be taken as an equal test by the reader.

The "trivial facts" of the plot are that Sir Roderick and Maria Shelley decide to send their fourteen-year-old daughter Clemence and their eleven-year-old son Sefton away to schools owned by relatives. To top off this family arrangement, Oliver Shelley, Sir Roderick's son by his first marriage, is to be a substitute music master at the boys' school for the same term that his half brother Sefton is a student.

When Clemence arrives at her school, she immediately undergoes an inquisitorial grilling from her dormitory mates Gwendolyn, Ethel, and Verity. Almost automatically, Clemence is pushed into lying about the wealth of her parents, the number of servants at home, and the extent of her wardrobe. This inauspicious beginning leads by gradual steps to Clemence's systematic cheating at school because of pressure from her parents to maintain a good record.

At the same time, Sefton undergoes a similar grilling at his school, in which his new friends refer to his mother, a second wife, as his father's "concubine," until the matron claps a lid on their enthusiastic ragging. Sefton, too, undertakes a consistent course of cheating by studying the masters' notes in their desks at night when the rest of the school is asleep.

At the adult level, the perversely brilliant Oliver too is investigated by his colleagues. While he has no recourse to cheating in his position as a master, he immediately falls into an intimate relationship with Oliver Spode, the mathematics master. This relationship causes a stern rebuke from Lucius Cassidy, Oliver Shelley's uncle and owner of the school.

At the time that Oliver is receiving his warning, both Sefton and Clemence have faced a panel of masters and mistresses to account for their misdeeds, and both are informed that their cheating must be brought to the attention of their parents. The climax of this set of events is the Christmas vacation when the owners of both schools are guests of the Shelley's. The rest of the novel is devoted to the revelation of various forms of dishonesty and abandonment to passion on the part of the adults, which balances the failings of the children in a perfect symmetry that is pointed out at the end of the novel.

While it would be impossible here to survey the entanglement of the adults' affairs in the same breathlessly meticulous fashion that it is done in the novel, the upshot is that Maria Shelley stole an earring, and that Sir Roderick and Mr. Firebrace (his former father-in-law) have both fathered illegitimate children. Mr. Firebrace's bastard son is Oliver Spode, the mathematics master, and thus the intimate relationship between him and Oliver Shelley is in reality one between uncle and nephew. Sir Roderick's illegitimate son is revealed to be Aldom, the butler, an intimate companion of Clemence and Sefton who delights them by his mimicry of various members of the household. The earrings have run throughout the entire entanglement because Mr. Firebrace gave one of them to Mrs. Spode when Oliver was born. The second one was stolen by Maria Shelley so she could get enough money to buy back for Sir Roderick a farm at the heart of his lands for which he has pined many years. But by a typically complex irony, he originally sold that very farm in order to compensate the mother of Aldom.

Thus Sir Roderick now knows his wife to be a polite thief, and she sees that he, as well as Mr. Firebrace, has been a philanderer. A subsidiary result of these wild oats is the involvement of Oliver Spode and Oliver Shelley in a kind of "incestuous" monosexual relationship.

At the conclusion, the parents have a chastened view of their children's "stumbles," having had to acknowledge their own. As in the end of a Greek tragedy, where the greatest gain is in what Aristotle called "discovery"—or knowledge of some fact that bears on the moral consequences of one's actions—so at the end of most Compton-Burnett novels, fuller knowledge of oneself and others is the fruit of the action. The wheel has come full circle. The farm is restored to Sir Roderick; the earrings are restored to the former owners; and Clemence and Sefton are happily at home again. But all these restorations are made with the knowledge of the depths of moral experience on the part of the characters. As the children sum up the result of their school interlude, they see with the eyes of their friends that their mother is shabby and that their father is simple; their governess cannot compare to professional teachers. And, conversely, their school friends see them as cheaters.

Just as Justine Gaveston and her brothers, at the conclusion of *A Family and a Fortune,* discuss the emotional purgation they felt as spectators to the action, so do Oliver, Clemence, and Sefton make a similar comment in the nursery scene that closes this novel. Oliver says:

"We can only hide our heads at home. Homes cause the shame, but they also provide a hiding-place for it, and we have to take one thing with another."
"You would hardly think homes would be so fair," said Clemence.
"No, we see the claim they have on us. And anyhow they impose it. You see life whole, Clemence, I leave you with a heavy heart, but with an easy mind."
"I suppose the same words would apply to us," said his sister, as the door closed.
"Well, anyhow we have nothing to dread now," said Sefton. "Everything seems to be over."
"That is what it is. There is nothing left. Nothing good, nothing bad, nothing to dread, nothing to hope for. Nothing." (310-11)

It is not accidental that Matthew Arnold's phrase about Sophocles should find its place in Oliver's speech, since the discussion is a very direct treatment of that ironically oblique justice which is all that tragedy grants us.

Aside from Lesbia Firebrace, the quietly avaricious, self-seeking, and self-satisfied owner of the girls' school, there is no real tyrant in this novel. In fact, the gentle benevolence of Sir Roderick and Maria comes almost as a relief from the family tensions common to most of the other novels. And, with the exception of Lesbia, most of the masters and mistresses at the school are congenial types; but their complacent lack of suspicion allows the children to cheat for a long period before they are discovered.

It is another matter with the school companions, who provide a wide range of moral types, descending to pure viciousness.

VIII *Conclusion*

In this group of novels—*Daughters and Sons, A Family and a Fortune, Parents and Children, Elders and Betters, Bullivant and the Lambs, Two Worlds and Their Ways*—Miss Compton-Burnett has continued to work with her accustomed brilliance, turning out a series of masterpieces in close succession. While there has been no diminution in the brittle and caustic wit of the dialogue, in the complexity of the plots, or in the variety of characterization, we find in these novels no major crimes of the order that typified the earlier novels. Nevertheless, there is enough petty meanness to enable us seriously to apply to these novels one of the hypocritical remarks of Josephine Napier that "what are called the little things are the gravest human wrongs."

Beginning with Muriel Ponsonby of *Daughters and Sons* and running through Nevill Sullivan of *Parents and Children*, Julius and Dora Calderon of *Elders and Betters,* Marcus and Jasper Lamb of *Bullivant and the Lambs,* to Clemence and Sefton Shelley of *Two Worlds and Their Ways,* Miss Compton-Burnett has explored a rich vein of childhood experience. While Muriel Ponsonby is largely remembered for her comic scenes, the other portraits are darker and deeper in implication, perhaps reaching a kind of nadir in the private religion of Julius and Dora and in the lifeless despair of Marcus and Jasper. The sympathy and fraternal affection of the older children has been a constant element running through from the first novel.

Another consistent new element in this group of novels is the author's preoccupation with balancing one age group, milieu, or class against another in a symmetry that is often one of the strongest structural forces in the novel. To be sure, the seeds of this method can be seen in the alternation between academic and domestic scenes in *Dolores* and in *Pastors and Masters,* and in the movements from one household to another in the suite of manor novels following these first two efforts. But never before has the author managed the contrasts with so many complex interrelated plot strains as she does in the contrasts between master and servant in *Bullivant and the Lambs.* In *Two Worlds and Their Ways* these contrasts are between domestic and academic concerns, but also necessarily between adults and children. In *A Family and a Fortune* this balancing of faults even reaches the proportions whereby the sin of the tyrant (Matty expelling Miss Griffin) is paralleled by a "stumble" in an essentially good character (Dudley Gaveston's flight from the house in a jealous rage). In general, the faults of the ladies vary considerably; the men are rather monotonously guilty of youthful fornication.

CHAPTER 4

Homes and Families

> "Well, most of us want something besides our
> homes and families."
> "That is how other homes and families come
> about," said Nigel.—*A Father and His Fate*

I *Familiar Patterns*

IVY Compton-Burnett's novels of the early 1950's show a
slackening of inventiveness and a tendency to continue in
familiar old patterns after some of the material has lost the
vivacity it had in earlier volumes. But the works are nevertheless
consistently interesting; and, where they are strong, they are as
strong as anything in the earlier works. *Darkness and Day*
(1951), for example, contains some of the most delightful verbal
fencing matches between children and governess found in any
of Miss Compton-Burnett's work. And the portrait of Cassius
Clare in *The Present and the Past* (1953) equals that of any
earlier tyrant.

For those readers who were delighted by the author's ex-
cursions into childhood in the novels of the late 1930's and the
1940's, *Mother and Son* (1955) stirred an unjustified hope that
Miss Compton-Burnett might expand her treatment of Plautus
the cat in that novel into later novels. While *A Father and His
Fate* (1957) deals with familiar materials, *A Heritage and Its
History* (1959) signals a new access of vitality and freshness;
it carries its characters through a span of time and a wealth of
developments unusual in all the author's work. *The Mighty and
Their Fall* (1961) concerns a chastening set of lessons administered to a father and daughter, both of whom at the end must
learn to live with each other's weaknesses. The lean simplicity
that characterizes this period is carried forward in *A God and
His Gifts* (1963) in which an indomitably passionate *pater-*

familias is repeatedly exposed before his family for philandering. If this novel reenacts many a situation from earlier volumes, the spareness of the dialogue nevertheless imparts a new kind of nobility to the interchanges between the characters.

II Darkness and Day

The references to Greek tragedy become far more explicit in *Darkness and Day* (1951) than in the earlier works. Here, too, a set of characters moves toward "discovery." One of them remarks: " 'Those who suffered from lack of knowledge have full knowledge now' " (260). This suffering from lack of knowledge consists of Bridget Lovat's mistaken conviction that her husband, Edmund, is also her father; the horror of the assumption led her to take her husband and two daughters into exile from the family. The novel opens with the return of Bridget with Edmund and their children Rose and Viola. They can no longer live alone with their secret; and, as they announce their dark knowledge to Edmund's mother Selina and his brother Gaunt, Bridget adds that at least she has not put her eyes out. Later Gaunt and Selina enlarge on this theme:

"Bridget has done and suffered the traditional tragic things. As nearly the same as Oedipus, as a woman could. He killed his father and married his mother. And she caused her mother's death when she was born, and married her father. The difference is, as she said herself, that she has not put out her eyes."

"Perhaps we are fortunate," said Selina drily. "Or perhaps fashions have changed. It does not seem that Oedipus was thought to have acted oddly under the circumstances. Or to have been felt exacting in requiring his daughter's attendance for the rest of his days. The children may not know how fortunate they are. But talking in this way does nothing for us. It does not alter the truth."

"And it is already a matter on a full scale. I hope Bridget is beyond the stage of the first impulsiveness. Oedipus lost no time in going the full length. Anything like that would make it very public. He seemed to think it proper for it to be that. He went about from town to town, talking about it. But I don't think Bridget would do that." (135-36)

There is no need for Bridget to do so, for her daughter Rose, who was reading a book on the floor, has listened to this entire conversation and immediately carries it to the servants. There follows a scene in which the ten-year-old and the eight-year-old give their own version of Oedipus to Fanshawe, the nurse.

After the protracted mysteries, the firm knowledge emerges that Edmund's illegitimate daughter is not his wife Bridget; she is Mildred Hallam, the housekeeper for Bridget's godfather, Sir Ransom Chace. And Bridget herself is Sir Ransom's illegitimate daughter by the Lovats' cook, Mrs. Spruce. The reason that the two women were confused is that both were adopted by a pair of cousins who had the same surname and Christian name. Thus the fear of incest that has hung over the mind of Bridget is revealed as an error, and the characters truly emerge from darkness to day, as the title indicates. This ending is actually the reverse of the tragic archetype, but it is in keeping with the author's frequently comic tendency.

This novel, coming so quickly on the heels of *Bullivant and the Lambs* and *Two Worlds and Their Ways*, raises the critical problem that has been mentioned before: the close resemblance between a train of novels. The two pendant revelations of illegitimate daughters in the Chace and Lovat households is directly reminiscent of Mr. Firebrace's and of Sir Roderick Shelley's illegitimate sons. Just as the latter's son is a butler, so Edmund Lovat's illegitimate daughter is a housekeeper for the Chace family. And the kitchen comedy of *Darkness and Day* is nearly a carbon copy of passages in *Bullivant and the Lambs*. Ambrose parallels Bullivant; Mrs. Spruce resembles Mrs. Selden, the cook; and Bartle is indistinguishable from George. The only nuance of difference is that Mrs. Spruce cannot be represented as so narrowly pious as Mrs. Selden, in view of her passionate involvement as a girl. And Bartle does not follow George in theft.

It must be added that *Darkness and Day* does exhibit distinctive qualities that set it apart from Miss Compton-Burnett's earlier novels. For one thing, the repeated references to darkness and light in the dialogue, especially in the early passages, give a poetic cohesion to the theme which is a new quality in Miss Compton-Burnett's writing. Moreover, the two children, Rose and Viola, are radically different from any of their predecessors. Their mother's somber preoccupation with the idea of incest and their father's inherent lack of interest in them have encouraged these girls to develop into wise and wily little savages.

[84]

Their direct rudeness, however, often consists simply of the candid attitude of the two strong-minded creatures who have never been touched by the refined tortures of civilized manners.

The scenes in which the children exhaust and defeat Mildred Hallam, their self-appointed governess, are among the most brilliantly comic in all the author's work. Mildred comes to them offering her patience and love as precious gifts; their persistence in ignoring her as they busy themselves with their paint boxes reduces her to sputtering rage. Then they deftly point out that her patience was a rather shallow gift. The dialectic by which they convert her proffered love into self-interest and boasting is somewhat more complex but equally maddening.

Their remarks about incest are necessarily limited by the range of their experience, but they vindicate themselves in discussing Sir Ransom's death. It is clear that he has transmitted to them his own peculiar brand of personal wisdom. When they are told of his death, the girls instinctively sense which of the adults feel genuine grief and which ones feel a spurious emotion. They reject the conventional view of the old man and his wife awaiting them in heaven as being far too similar to the workhouse. And their logic is unassailable when they decide that, if he and his wife *are* looking down from such a dreary heaven, the only duty they have is to amuse him by being as naughty as possible. Then they twist the knife in the wound by adding that this naughtiness will be an act of selfless devotion!

We see the traits that Rose and Viola inherited when Sir Ransom blasphemously gives his own version of a passage from the Book of Common Prayer on his deathbed: "'There is not much that I do regret. I have done much that I ought to have done. Much that I ought not to have done, I would do again. That is true of most of us. Remorse is the result of a change of mood, not a change of nature'" (244-45).

Gaunt Lovat, the bachelor brother of Edmund, is as avaricious of gossip as Julian Wake of *Brothers and Sisters*. It is his irrepressible need to see Sir Ransom's will before the funeral that also exposes letters and photographs which prove Bridget's parentage. He, too, adds the only grimly comic touch to Bridget's early assertion of having married her father: he systematically catalogs the now double-jointed family relationships. The family quickly suppresses him when he threatens to perform the same service on learning that Mildred Hallam, the Chace housekeeper and the Lovat governess, is the daughter of Edmund.

Miss Compton-Burnett's typical symmetries continue to abound in this volume. Just as the Chace household is led by Sir Ransom, eighty-eight, so the Lovat household is dominated by Selina, seventy-eight; there is a subtle counterpoint in attitudes toward death on the part of these two elderly parents that is played off against the attitudes of their children. Sir Ransom has two daughters, Selina two sons. A smoldering fight between Emma, the older Chace daughter, and Mildred, the housekeeper, is paralleled in the Lovat menage by an undercurrent of resentment between Selina and her daughter-in-law Bridget.

III The Present and the Past

On the last page of *The Present and the Past* (1953), one of the minor characters, who has been merely a spectator, refers to it as a "sad tale." Indeed, it is one of Miss Compton-Burnett's saddest, and in that respect it resembles *Men and Wives* (1931). Like Harriet Haslam of the earlier novel, Cassius Clare makes a hypocritically false suicide attempt which his family meets with consternation. When he does die shortly afterwards from a heart condition, his relatives experience as piercing a regret as Harriet's family, without the consolation that the Haslam children found carrying out the dead tyrant's wishes. Cassius asked nothing of his family except that they flatter him and sympathize with him when his personality offered no grounds for this attention. Such a colorless man elicited only exasperation from his dependents. When he is gone, they are left with the sober knowledge that they ignored him and that, if he were to return, he would make the same demands and they would answer them in the same way.

Although we shall see that *The Present and the Past* fails in several ways, the portrait of Cassius Clare is a triumph of characterization. He is a man without distinction who whines and carps incessantly; he cannot even carry out his self-pitying threat to eat nothing at breakfast, except on the day of his death. He pettily denigrates all the laudable qualities in those about him, but at the same time he demands a silly inflation of his own imaginary virtues.

Despite all these failings, however, he emerges as an authentically pitiable person, not as an exaggerated caricature. All the pain he inflicts on others is really unintentional, and since the rest of the family have greater sensitivity and insight than he, they have the double burden of trying to accept him for what he is at the same time that they must pander to what he thinks he is. That they fail at this task and that they regret their failure bitterly is the tragedy of many such a situation in life. The miraculous effect of Miss Compton-Burnett's technique is that the reader accepts the complexity of value for what it is, without judging harshly.

Cassius's most monstrous act is to permit his divorced first wife, Catherine, to break the pact on which she parted from him—that she would never again see her two sons. This novel, thus, is a good illustration of the place of manners in Miss Compton-Burnett's work; for the return of a former wife to a small country village presents to her husband and to his present wife questions of social form that are hardly conceived of in traditional etiquette. His present wife Flavia insistently points out to Cassius the unsuitability of his decisions, and his father, the elderly Mr. Clare, seconds her with his quietly devastating one-line remarks. Cassius, however, is flattered to think that in having two wives together, he can survey his "harem." He has no further thought of how he is capitalizing on Catherine's maternal desperation, nor of how he is violating the position of Flavia. The deepest wounds, though, are inflicted on Fabian and Guy, Catherine's sons; having already adjusted themselves to a stepmother, they are now forced to reevaluate their loyalties in a decision that repeatedly reduces Guy to anguished tears.

What is more, Cassius insists on a general family gathering to witness Catherine's encounter with her sons, from whom she has been estranged for nine years. Chapter VII, in which this meeting occurs, is a compendium of all the unspeakable remarks that such a situation might produce, all of them finding full expression on the lips of Cassius and his innocent children. His mind is so opaque that he actually thinks he can ask the children—before their real mother and their stepmother—whom they love the most; and the clear implication is that he wishes his name to be the answer.

The unhappy result of the situation is that Flavia and Catherine become very close friends, almost to the total exclusion of Cassius from their lives and those of their children. In a typical reaction, Cassius takes four tablets from his father's jar of medicine, knowing very well that it would require ten to kill a man. The family is shocked at the spiritual desperation that would lead to suicide until the three-year-old Toby finds the bottle. Toby's action reveals that it was a totally crass appearance at suicide done only to elicit sympathy and attention. Then the two wives and the children deal with him sharply; nearly all of them in turn tell him—at his own request—that they think his act dishonest and despicable.

The Present and the Past is a relatively short novel; and, while the major plot situation evokes a deep, somber emotion, the minor figures are handled in a somewhat perfunctory manner. For example, Bennett and Miss Ridley, the children's nurse and governess, are sketched in so summarily that they hardly seem to carry their own weight. But there is also a weakening in the kitchen comedy; Ainger, the butler, resembles the Bullivant prototype, except that he is given to boasting about his indispensable role as a friend to the master, something Bullivant would find in poor taste, because his need would be self-evident. Ainger *might* carry this off if he had more force as an individual personality, but that is exactly what he lacks. Mrs. Frost, the cook, and the housemaids are drab figures. Instead of a boy helper on the pattern of George and Bartle, we have the elderly Thomas Halliday, an engagingly plainspoken cynic. The servants have no plot function, except that Ainger helps Mr. Clare to decide not to send for the doctor after Cassius's second illness.

The children of Cassius and Flavia, by contrast, are clearly delineated, individualized persons. Toby Clare carries on in the tradition of Muriel Ponsonby and Nevill Sullivan. While Toby's speech traits are his own, he shows Nevill's inability to cope with personal pronouns; in his obsessive egotism, he displays the undisciplined savagery of early childhood. Like Nevill, however, he has his direct effect on adult affairs. This makes an ironic contrast between the toy-minded simplicity of the son and the hypocritical complexity of the father who was only shamming suicide. Henry and Megan are diametrically opposed in attitudes toward their father, although they are close to each other; Henry cannot forgive Cassius for his moody infliction of pain on others, whereas Megan, who is the victim of many of Cassius's gibes, shows a magnanimous breadth of sympathy for her father.

Although Miss Compton-Burnett's work is as far removed as possible from the typically symbolic romantic novel, the opening scene of this book bears remarkable—if accidental—resemblance to many a scene in D. H. Lawrence's *Women in Love*. In this work, Lawrence is fond of pointing out parallels between the behavior of animals and corresponding human beings. At the outset of *The Present and the Past*, one of the author's most memorable scenes is the visit of the Clare children to the chicken yard. Here Toby tries to feed cake to a sick hen which the others are pecking mercilessly. As the children watch the process, their comments on the ruthlessness of nature, supplemented by the more callous remarks of the servants, bear closely on their own experience of family tyranny. After the other chickens have heedlessly stepped on the body of the hen that died hungry and thirsty, the governess's allusion to Darwin comes with chilling effect. While the resemblance to Lawrence is entirely fortuitous, it is one of those curious outcroppings that demonstrate the universality of human experience which overrides the barriers of literary schools and techniques.

IV Mother and Son

Cassius's bad manners are based on a lack of perception; Miranda Hume, the eighty-year-old tyrant of *Mother and Son* (1955), is much closer to Sophia Stace, Sabine Ponsonby, Josephine Napier, and Sukey Donne—the great line of securely powerful matriarchs and aunts who practice *noblesse oblige* with reverse English. They revel in their power with such greed that they need to test it hourly by outrageous violations of the social fabric. Miranda opens this novel with a brilliant display by requiring her niece, nephews, son, and husband to remain in the room while she interviews a Miss Burke for the post of her companion in a ruthless, cutting, and overbearing manner. Her complete omniscience in the household is such that she unfailingly enters every room just at the moment that one of her pet rules is being violated.

As we have seen, conspicuous failure in decency of manners is often indicative of much more profound moral shortcomings. When Miranda knows herself close to death, her husband Julius very selfishly and ill-advisedly confesses to her that Alice, Francis, and Adrian—his supposed niece and nephews whom they have reared—are in reality his illegitimate children. The affair that produced them was a consequence of Miranda's morbid attachment to their son Rosebery (indicated by the title to the novel) which excluded Julius from the family. This eleventh-hour confession hastens Miranda's death, and Julius's ineptness is roundly condemned by Rosebery.

But when Rosebery goes to look at Miranda's will, the inevitable hidden letter and photograph come to light, revealing that Rosebery, too, is illegitimate. All the tragic spite in Miranda's dying speech now rings falsely; if Julius bumbled by revealing his sin to his wife at the worst possible moment, she made a far more egregious moral error in assuming that she was above the need to confide her own failing.

This symmetrical revelation of extramarital relations on the part of both husband and wife recalls the balancing of faults in the group of "diptych" novels treated in the preceding chapter, but never before has a Compton-Burnett gentlewoman been found capable of this kind of stumble. The Victorian assumption was that only men succumb to the urgency of sexual passion.

In the meantime, the rejected would-be companion Miss Burke takes a position in the neighborhood as housekeeper to two confirmed spinsters, Emma Greatheart and Hester Wolsey. Shortly after this, Hester's investments fail; she applies for the position as Miranda Hume's companion, with more success than Miss Burke. When Miranda dies, Julius becomes engaged to Emma, and Rosebery asks for the hand of Miss Burke. Hester is at the center of the whole development, for her position in the Hume household creates the intercourse between the families. Because she is a dedicated spinster and is jealous of the loss of her friend Emma, she reveals to the whole assembled family, including the children, that Julius has not confided his entire past to Emma. The consequent revelation of Julius's philandering is enough to turn Emma from marrying him, and when she reestablishes her household with Hester, she also makes a pro-

vision for Miss Burke, who was planning to marry the selfish
and demanding Rosebery simply to provide for her old age.
At the end of the novel, we find the two households reconsti-
tuted exactly as at the beginning, with the difference that the
Humes have lost Miranda and the spinsters have gained Miss
Burke.

The weakness in the plot is that Hester had to know about
the family skeletons in some way or other in order to blast the
engagements by her revelation. The author chose to have Hester
overhear each of the family sessions in which the sins came to
light. Miss Compton-Burnett's readers, as we have seen in other
situations, accustom themselves to rather strong coincidences,
but this one must be hard for even the most seasoned devotee
to swallow.

The children in this novel represent an average set of char-
acterizations; Alice and Francis are leagued by a sympathy that
somewhat excludes the tearful and bookish Adrian. In their
whispered—but audible—bitternesses, they exasperate the adults
as do most of the children in Compton-Burnett novels. Their
pitched and spiteful battles with the tutor, Mr. Pettigrew, are
wickedly amusing in themselves, although they lose a bit of
luster by comparison with how Viola and Rose dealt with Miss
Hallam in *Darkness and Day*. The tutor's fawning ways and his
mean curiosity about family secrets, allied with an inflated
view of his own social position, recall Mr. Penrose of *A Family
and a Fortune*.

One of the most striking new developments in this novel is
the prominence given to Plautus, Hester and Emma's cat.
Logically enough, he is named after a Latin writer whose plays
were not very good—and Plautus, too, has written no good plays!
The meager hints given by the author indicate that he is a
very ordinary cat, but his value in the novel lies in the pre-
posterous talents, moods, and faculties ascribed to him by the
two spinsters.

The two households are also distinguished by memorable
human portraits in the persons of Rosebery Hume and Hester
Wolsey, both eccentric and complex persons. One might suspect
that Rosebery is meant as a projection of what Gregory Haslam
of *Men and Wives* will become as an adult. Gregory, almost

morbidly devoted to a domineering mother, is deeply absorbed in feminine interests; Rosebery, too, spends every waking moment in his mother's company, even refusing to let the hired companion usurp his privilege of reading Miranda to sleep at bedtime. He is also attracted to other women on an essentially feminine basis, and he feels the same tensions as Gregory in this treason to his mother. Rosebery's devotion, unlike Gregory's, is perhaps a bit more understandable since his Oedipal hostility to Julius may be based on an instinctual feeling of the truth that he is, indeed, the son of another man.

Hester Wolsey, the spinster who recognizes, at least in part, the kind of substitute love she lavishes on Plautus, is a pendant figure to Rosebery. Hester is fiercely proud of her independence, and when her investments fail, she would rather leave Emma than become a dependent on her friend's largess. But when her employment leads to the engagements of Emma and Miss Burke, Hester singlehandedly breaks up the arrangements by publicly revealing the secret of Julius Hume's past. She is so totally dedicated to spinsterhood that she finally bows to accepting Emma's support in order to reestablish their menage. She, too, significantly refused one of Rosebery's earlier proposals.

Although both Hester and Rosebery would be adjudged somewhat abnormal by the more fashionable American psychiatrists, the British have not yet absorbed all of our conformist criteria of "adjustment," "emotional stability," and "peer group approval." Like Virginia Woolf's treatment of Septimus Warren Smith in *Mrs. Dalloway*, Miss Compton-Burnett's approach is completely free from preconceptions or canned value judgments. She never betrays by so much as a raised eyebrow that either Rosebery or Hester is anything but one other human creature to be taken on the same terms as all other persons. To be sure, Hester's and Rosebery's own values become clear as soon as they appear in the novel, but the advantages and disadvantages of their ways of life are neither sentimentalized nor condemned, except in the natural ways that other characters within the novel could be expected to react. The bland good taste of this treatment is one of the highest achievements of British civilization; it involves complete respect for the variety of human motives and the sanctity of individual self-determination.

V A Father and His Fate

A Father and His Fate (1957) offers nothing new in terms of essential plot or characterization; but the lively sparkle and bite of the dialogue are at Ivy Compton-Burnett's highest level, with a fresh nuance in tone. The conversations of this novel have a carping, bickering character that exasperates more than one character within the novel, but it seldom fails to delight the reader.

The basic plot is a variation on the Enoch Arden situation of *Parents and Children* (1941), except that in this case both the husband and wife, Miles and Ellen Mowbray, leave on a voyage to attend to family business, and only the husband is rescued from a shipwreck. Shortly after his return, he wrests Verena Gray, a friend of his sister-in-law, away from her engagement to his nephew Malcolm and into his own house. A week before their marriage it is revealed that Ellen was rescued from the shipwreck, too, and has been recovering in a neighboring village. After her return it is learned that Miles knew of her presence —just as Ridley Cramner knew that Fulbert Sullivan had not been lost—and was sending her money in the hope that she would stay away.

Verena, who resembles Camilla Bellamy of *Men and Wives* (1931) in her fierce determination to get what she wants, immediately marries her former fiancé, Malcolm; but she remains in the household as an irritating reminder of Miles's failure to remain loyal to Ellen. It is by Verena's agency that Miles's sending money to the absent Ellen is brought to the attention of the family. But Miles's newfound devotion to Ellen and the hostility of the entire family to Verena are too strong for even her will. She leaves with a brilliant, long oration which recalls Hetta Ponsonby's in *Daughters and Sons* (1937), one of those immensely satisfying moments when a character is permitted to give the entire assembled family an account of his own motives as well as what he thinks of the family and of their actions over a long period.

Verena reveals that she will give Malcolm cause to divorce her, and that she will send their child—when it is born—to him when he remarries. At the very end of the book, Nigel and

Rudolf, Miles's two brilliant and caustic nephews, learn by means of some compromising nightclothes that Verena left in Ellen's bedroom, that Verena's child was fathered by Miles before Ellen's return rather than by Malcolm. Verena's quick marriage to Malcolm was, therefore, merely a means of legitimizing the baby. As the novel closes, we see the boys imparting this information to their nurse, Miss Manders, and thus to the entire village.

For the seasoned Compton-Burnett reader, this novel makes its strongest appeal in the contrasts to be observed between the character of Miles Mowbray and his widowed sister-in-law Eliza, who lives with her two sons in a neighboring house. They are both tyrants—within the conventional definition of tyranny in these novels—but with completely different styles. They demonstrate succinctly the typical differences between male and female tyranny as explained in the introductory chapter of this study.

Miles Mowbray, a coward at heart, is unable to deal with Nigel and Rudolf; he finally resorts to ordering them out of his house since he cannot compete with them in a battle of wits and cannot bear to allow them to titter to themselves when he is present. He is hardly any better in dealing with his own daughters. And yet, like many cowards, he shows an infinite resourcefulness in finding excuses to gloss over his own moral failings. As his family remarks, there is something extraordinary about so much cowardice combined with such a thick skin; he wriggles out of a series of showdowns that are so monstrous in their implications that neither his wife nor his daughters can even bring themselves to think through all the base moral implications.

By contrast, Eliza is an inconceivably self-centered, power-mad, domineering woman, who frightens Miles nearly to death. She shows up with absolute regularity at his home, always uninvited, whenever there is a crisis. In this, she is reminiscent of Matty Seaton of *A Family and a Fortune* (1939). Eliza and Miles have in common the habit of appearing as neglected and pitiable parents; because she does not have Miles's hope of remarrying, she lavishes her fiercely destructive love on Malcolm, who has been named Miles's heir and who thus escapes Eliza's domination for weeks at a time, and on Nigel and Rudolf, whom she commands as if they were the most abject lackeys.

When Malcolm begins to show an interest in her protegée, Verena Gray, Eliza's opposition to the match rises nearly to the bitterness and spite of Josephine Napier when her nephew Simon fell in love with Ruth, also a protegée of the tyrant.

At the outset, it was noted that *A Father and His Fate* is distinguished by the incessant bickering tone of conversation. This is particularly evident in the interchanges between Malcolm and his cousin Constance, which often attain the qualities of stichomythia that Mr. Liddell attributes to some of the dialogue. The most acutely painful of these interchanges occurs after the supposed death of Ellen, Constance's mother. Constance makes the standard theological assumptions about the continued life of her mother's soul, whereas Malcolm is closer to the author's own values in his skeptical attitude. Whether we call him "pagan," "agnostic," or "doubting," it is simple, empirical truth that he defends. It is usually Constance who is shown up as contradictory in thought, and it is always she who leaves the room in exasperation or pique.

Even though Constance is usually bested in these interchanges, Miss Compton-Burnett does not allow us to condescend. When it becomes a question of the daughters' speaking to the father about his unseemly behavior with a girl forty-four years younger than he, Ursula and Audrey, who have been far more sympathetic than Constance heretofore, entirely fail in courage. It is Constance who confronts their father and who speaks out. When this conversation has no effect on Miles, it is again Constance who speaks plainly to Verena, who in her own way is a far more formidable opponent. Even Malcolm, the wronged fiancé of Verena, cannot bring himself to utter a word during these interviews. After both attempts fail, Audrey and Ursula rightly point out that a major part of Constance's motive in speaking was that of playing the role of outraged virtue, of seeing herself as a moral crusader. As reprehensible as that trait may be, especially in the Compton-Burnett constellation of values, it remains that Constance is able to do a good deed when all the "good" characters are overcome by embarrassment. Constance obviously resembles Justine Gaveston of *A Family and a Fortune* (1939) in the demonstration that while it takes a small mind and a tough hide to face up to the tyrants, these failings can be accounted downright virtues in the world as we know it.

Malcolm becomes involved in bickering of the same quality
when he visits his mother; in these cases, he seems even more
in the right than in his talks with Constance, since he speaks
truths to an overbearing woman who has never before been
opposed by her sons. The situation is a faint recall of Matthew
Haslam's exchanges with his mother, since they also concerned
the mother's opposition to the son's marriage. But of all the
male characters in the novels, Malcolm most nearly resembles
Grant Edgeworth of *A House and Its Head* (1935), with whose
situation his has a large number of similarities.

VI A Heritage and Its History

Reviewers have referred to Miss Compton-Burnett in the
metaphor of a wine that improves with age; fortuitously, too,
1959 was considered an especially good year in French vineyards.
Certainly *A Heritage and Its History*, her novel of that year, is
one of her finest. Very important plot developments burgeon
throughout the length of this novel, so that there are never any
stretches where one feels the characters are speaking about
topics of general concern simply to fill up space. The charac-
terizations are subtle, with at least two or three very profound
evolutions of personality throughout the course of the book. The
dialogue itself is of the highest quality, with a consistent emphasis on dramatic irony, in the sense in which the term is
applied to Greek tragedy. After one of these scenes, a character
who has full knowledge remarks on the matter: " 'It was like
a Greek tragedy,' said Walter. 'With people saying things with
a meaning they did not know, or with more meaning than they
knew. It is not the first today. Will it always be like this?' "[1]
By the time the reader has finished the novel, he can confidently
answer "Yes" to Walter's question. If there is any development
in the style, the dialogue seems even more ruthlessly abstract
than in many a preceding novel, with a granitelike nobility that
recalls many Sophoclean tragic utterances.

A Heritage and Its History is also distinctive in its broad
scope; this novel covers the life of three generations of the Challoner family over a period of more than thirty years; there are
several jumps in time of the sort that have been encountered
heretofore only between the first and second chapters of *Brothers*

and Sisters. New characters are introduced as late as the penultimate chapter. In a wide range of human types Simon, the
tyrant, is strongly contrasted with Sir Edwin, his uncle, who
dies in his nineties, and with Claud and Emma, two of the
most fiendish of Compton-Burnett infants.

The history of this heritage is a complex one that unrolls
with familiar kinds of developments. Simon Challoner is deeply
attached to the estate owned by his uncle, Sir Edwin, who,
despite his sixty-nine years, marries Rhoda Graham to fill the
gap left by the death of his brother. As one might expect from
a similar situation in *A House and Its Head* (1935), Rhoda
eventually bears Simon a child, which is acknowledged by Sir
Edwin as his own. This bars Simon from the inheritance. In his
searing bitterness at this ironic justice, Simon marries Rhoda's
sister Fanny and fathers five children whom he rears under an
iron discipline that features frequent threats of ending in the
workhouse.

This situation continues long enough for Simon's daughter
Naomi to fall hopelessly in love with his illegitimate son Hamish,
since the two think they are simply cousins. When they force
the issue of their impending engagement, Simon must call the
entire family together to announce to the three generations that
Hamish is in reality his son by his aunt, Rhoda, and that thus
Hamish and Naomi are in reality half brother and sister, with
the added complication that their mothers are sisters. This is
another instance of the fulldress public scene like Hetta Ponsonby's and Verena Gray's in which past moral escapades are
aired to the family.

Hamish vows he will never manage the estate himself, but
during a long trip he falls away from his ideal of disappointed
celibacy and brings back Marcia, a wife eleven years older than
he. Almost as if Simon were perversely fated to have liaisons
with the wives of the owners of the estate, he and Marcia have
a brief relation, this time without issue. But by an added irony,
it is this liaison which restores his hopes, since Marcia then
influences Hamish to renounce the estate in Simon's favor.

When Simon's lifelong hopes are finally confirmed, he undergoes a total change of character, and his children, accustomed
to hourly harshness from their father, experience the same fears
the Lamb children did on Horace's reform. The book ends on

the equivocal note of the children's fear that their father may revert to type; but even if he does continue in his newly found sunniness of outlook, they feel (even more equivocally) that they are the better for having suffered a blighted childhood.

In the standard range of topics for Compton-Burnett dialogue, there is relatively little variation; in this novel, however, there seems to be a greater emphasis on the subjects of death, ways of facing death, and intimations of mortality. As a rarely heard, but deeply satisfying, undertone, the curt remarks of Deakin, the dour butler, add a flavor of extreme cynicism that seems to set off the talk of death as fairly cheerful.

There seem to be subtle marks of changed intention on the part of the author here and there, which were perhaps not erased because the original lines were so felicitously sketched in. Rhoda and Fanny Graham, for example, are given rather full and piquant development when they are introduced in Chapter II. When they become spouses of the Challoner men, their characters become submerged; and all we hear of them is about their rather diluted sisterly devotion. But in the first view, they were sharply contrasted persons whose differences promised scenes of sharp repartee.

Marcia's affair with Simon late in the novel, although it is supported by ample hints and perceptions on the part of the children, is rather faintly delineated. What is worse, its moral implications for his wife and children—and their view of him— are ignored.

Emma, at two, is the youngest child of any consequence to appear in the novels; her first debut at a family luncheon is a marvel of understatement. Perhaps only Hemingway, in a story like "Hills Like White Elephants," is the equal of Miss Compton-Burnett in making monosyllables speak full eloquence.

Emma's older brothers and sister—Ralph, Graham, and Naomi —provide the standard adolescent chorus of whispered wickedness, with the usual maddening effects on the adults. Walter Challoner, Simon's brother, is paired off as the older Hamish was with Sir Edwin; Walter is in his own right a poet manqué who was sent down from Oxford, the genial uncle who modestly observes the actions and attitudes of his more active contemporaries. He is a refuge of sympathy for the young people.

Sir Edwin, like Sir Ransom of *Darkness and Day*, embodies

that peculiarly opaque and glazed wisdom of extreme age. Without hope or enthusiasm, but not yet ready to renounce life entirely, the aged live out their days, enjoying as much as anything the discomfiture which their longevity causes those about them. They present difficult passages for the children since the respect due to them would ordinarily call for extremely polished manners, but their avaricious feeling for the very young makes a bridge of sympathy that bypasses social observances. In both cases, the deathbed scenes are the most acute crises in manners.

In its general course, the plot is a sophisticated variation on the "false scent" variety. Simon's profound dedication to the estate is frustrated by his uncle's longevity, by his own wild oats, and by Hamish's several vacillations about how to dispose of the heritage. The whole business, despite the technically "comic" outcome, has a tragic tone. Most of the characters—particularly Hamish and Naomi—have gained, for all their pains, only knowledge of themselves and of others. It is one of the primary paradoxes of tragedy that knowledge is the greatest possible good at the same time that it is the least consoling reward in terms of our wills.

VII The Mighty and Their Fall

The same stable, unchanged outcome of a muddled state of affairs characterizes *The Mighty and Their Fall* (1961). Ninian Middleton, a widower, attempts to remarry in the face of full opposition on the part of his children. They are led by Lavinia, the oldest daughter, who is almost abnormally devoted to her father. When he finds she has suppressed a letter from Teresa, his fiancée, in the hope that his delay in answering will prevent the marriage, he exposes Lavinia before the entire family.

This impasse is partially relieved by the return of Ransom, Ninian's younger brother who has earned a fortune in distant parts and by apparently devious means. Close to death because of a weak heart, he sets up a separate household nearby, partially as a shelter for the disgraced Lavinia, where he plays an embarrassing ruse on Ninian to rebalance the scales in Lavinia's favor. He asks Ninian—just as Aunt Sukey Donne asked Anna in *Elders and Betters*—to destroy a will that would reward Ninian and to preserve one that would leave the fortune to

Lavinia. Ninian—again like Anna Donne—does the opposite, and
he is also exposed before the younger members of the family.

Now that the "stumbles" of father and daughter are equal,
Ransom dies, leaving Lavinia the money; she decides to marry
Hugo, an adopted son of the dead husband of Selina, the
mother of Ninian and Ransom. From page 15, Hugo's first
introduction, the practiced reader has assumed that Hugo is an
illegitimate son, so it is no surprise when Selina announces this
fact in order to prevent Lavinia's marrying him. But Hugo
proves Selina (and the practiced reader) wrong by thoroughly
investigating his own background. The reason Selina's husband
kept Hugo's childhood a mystery is that he had killed Hugo's
father in a seizure of "youthful violence." Now that the path
to marriage is clear, Selina dies, leaving a large provision to
Hugo in the certain knowledge that—if he has enough to satisfy
his full, selfish, bachelor independence—he will no longer want
to marry Lavinia. Thus the matriarch in this instance shows an
omniscience that extends beyond her death.

Lavinia reconciles herself to her father, and life resumes its
dull course, much to the disappointment of the eavesdropping
butler, Ainger, and Cook, who have become accustomed to the
excitement of daily crises.

At first Lavinia appears to be unscrupulous and selfish in
her violation of her father's correspondence; but then Ransom's
sympathy for her, even if he is the black sheep, leads to Ninian's
suppression of the will. If the reader feels righteously that Lavinia with her newfound wealth ought to abandon such a father,
he is disenchanted by her ultimate happy decision to return to
her father's house. This is the prevailing moral of all these
novels: none of us has a right to sit in judgment on others unless
we have undergone similar temptations ourselves—and, if we
have, we have almost certainly fallen victim to them.

In Selina, Ninian, and Lavinia, we see the dilemma of three
likeminded members of a family who have to live with each
other. Between Selina and Ninian there is an easy truce since
her son renders to her all the respect and honor due a superannuated tyrant who has eight children and grandchildren on
whom to practice her power; she allows him to have the final
word in management of the estate, and she pays lip service to
his prerogative as a male head of the household. Their powers

are well enough balanced so that they complement each other. It is Lavinia who has the problems of adjustment and who has inherited enough obstinacy from Selina and Ninian to make them uncomfortable too. Even though she is twenty, she has been kept in complete—if affectionate—subjugation by Ninian. This has emphasized her childlike qualities. When Ninian's threatened remarriage cuts into Lavinia's province, she immediately and unscrupulously acts, just as Ninian does with Ransom's will and just as Ransom himself does in tricking Ninian.

In descending order of their ages, the dependent figures become the more formidable. Hugo is by his own admission without a trace of manliness or courage, and he refuses the two opportunities for marriage that present themselves. He is one of a large company of fainéant and self-indulgent bachelors that people these works. By contrast, Egbert, the elder son who is studying at Oxford, is a temporary dependent who will one day manage the estate himself. In a sense, he is a pendant character to Lavinia (to whom he is fiercely loyal) since he will ultimately become an active, rather than an observant, person. But, unlike Lavinia, as long as Ninian is alive he has no rights at the moment; and the sureness of his inheritance is paid for by the sureness of his submission until that time. He nevertheless consistently annoys Ninian by the precision of his ethical distinctions in commenting on his father's actions.

Egbert's younger sister Agnes is an unassuming creature whose quietness covers an appalling capacity to love Selina, when the rest of the family assume that Selina would cow even God Himself on Judgment Day. Agnes's is perhaps the most complete servitude in the whole family, for her love for Selina is simply a refraction of Selina's finding her the favorite among the children.

Hengist and Leah, eleven and ten years old, are precisely at the age when they begin to comprehend adult affairs enough to mask their understanding by an assumed innocence. This protective coloring frees them to make the most outrageous remarks about death, marriage, love, and money, with what amounts to complete impunity. Their governess, Miss Starkie, suffers the traditional tortures of her lot; on the one hand, she must pretend that her influence is a factor in improving the children simply to retain her position; but, on the other hand, their behavior in front of the adults consistently belies this assumption. In the meantime, the children carry on their own guerrilla warfare by snickering at her appetite, her unmarried state, and her inferior social position. If Miss Starkie has any reason to be thankful, it is that the Middleton children are not so precocious as the Sullivans in exposing gaps in her education.

The servants of this novel are a pale reflection of some of their predecessors. Ainger, the butler, bears the same name as his counterpart in *The Present and the Past;* his only distinctive characteristic is an avariciousness for gossip which he satisfies by listening at the doors during family discussions. Although Cook accompanies him in this pleasure whenever she can, her nonconformist piety, like that of Mrs. Selden in *Bullivant and the Lambs,* requires her to deplore too open a recognition of her curiosity. There are very sketchy conflicts with the butler's helper James, who insists on being called by his actual name of Percival, much to everyone's consternation.

Again, as in *The Present and the Past,* one wonders why the author bothered to include the kitchen comedy in *The Mighty* since it has no relation to the major plot. Moreover, the servants have absolutely no bearing on anything else in the book, except for the unusual final scene. In it Ainger and Cook discuss the events that have occurred, with several ironic twists on the words of the title, "the mighty and their fall." This ending gives an unaccustomed poetic finality to the novel.

VIII   A God and His Gifts

In her nineteenth novel, *A God and His Gifts* (1963), Miss Compton-Burnett returns to the situation of *Daughters and Sons* (1937), in which a hard-working novelist has gained immense popularity and has saved the family estate by renouncing his traditional leisure. Hereward Egerton, the ironical "God" of the title, resembles his predecessor, John Ponsonby, in his assumption that this renunciation frees him from ordinary conventions. Hereward is also annoyed by rivalry within the family, although his son Merton never has the success as a writer that John Ponsonby's daughter France gains.

Hereward, who has had a mistress, Rosa, marries Ada Merton in a rather perfunctory manner; after the birth of several children he becomes involved in a liaison with his sister-in-law, Emmeline, who is therefore sent away. Some years later, after Merton, the son of Hereward and Ada, has announced his engagement, Hereward begins secretly to show attention to Hetty, his daughter-in-law-to-be. The fatherhood of their illegitimate child is kept a close secret, and Merton, not suspecting that it is his father who has preceded him in his wife's affections, marries Hetty. Hereward nevertheless manages to adopt the child, Henry, another of the author's devastatingly egocentric young children.

Another son, Reuben, announces his engagement to Trissie, a fellow teacher from his school, and Hereward again begins to show embarrassingly intimate attentions to his future daughter-in-law. Reuben, who has by this time guessed about Hereward and Hetty, is thus forced to reveal to the whole family the secret about Henry's parentage. A third crisis occurs when Ada's sister Emmeline returns with her supposedly adopted daughter Viola, who was in reality fathered by Hereward. When the eldest son, Salomon, begins to fall in love with Viola, he warns his father that he does not want Hereward to show to Viola the attentions he showed to Hetty and to Trissie, the wives of the other two brothers. Since Salomon and Viola are half brother and sister, and since their mothers are sisters, Hereward is forced to reveal that he is the father of Viola in order to prevent the incestuous union. In the penultimate chapter, by a very weak plot device, Ada finally discovers evidence of her husband's affair with Rosa before he married Ada, so that all his philandering is now family property. The novel draws to a close with the death of Sir Michael, Hereward's father. At the very end, a wry note is sounded in Henry's announcement that when he grows up he will marry Maud, the daughter of Merton and Hetty. In his childish innocence, he does not realize she is his half sister and that his father is her grandfather.

Although we have seen that many of Miss Compton-Burnett's men hold themselves superior to moral law, Hereward far outdistances such figures as Simon Challoner of *A Heritage and Its History* in his indefatigable attentions to mistress, sister-in-law, and daughters-in-law. The complexity of family interrelationships is far greater in *A God and His Gifts* than in such a work as William Faulkner's *Absalom, Absalom!,* which, like its biblical namesake and like many a Greek tragedy, also deals in the problems of a father who has through his own unrestrained energy founded a dynasty which falls to ruin by internal contradictions. But Hereward's adulterous marathon is far too monstrous to be regarded in detail or with the kind of fascinated intensity that Faulkner lavishes on his characters. It is here that Miss Compton-Burnett's almost undernourished "late" manner shows to its greatest advantage. The novel is stripped of that luxuriance of minor characters and parallel subplots that allowed, in earlier novels, for elaborately discursive conversations about the doings in the manor. The relative simplicity of the book in this respect is paralleled by the stiffened formality, the abstractness, and the radical plainness of the dialogue.

In terms of characterization, Hereward's loyal sister, Zillah, and his aunt, Penelope Merton (who is equally devoted to her brother Alfred), are very pale sketches based on the model of Hetta Ponsonby of *Daughters and Sons,* but they have so few speeches in the novel that they are nearly negligible as characters. They may, like Rhoda and Fanny Graham of *A Heritage and Its History,* mark a change in the author's intention as she worked along, since the first introduction of each in the novel promises more importance than either is accorded in the course of the book. Alfred Merton, Hereward's father-in-law, appears simply as the traditional dispenser of wise advice. When he expressed his doubts about the advisability of Ada's marrying Hereward, Ada offered a vivacious counterargument. As if she bitterly learned the mistake in that action, she acquiesces in Alfred's later counsel to stand by Hereward despite his frequent betrayals of their marriage.

Given such a stripped-down, simplified form, it is only logical that the sounding board for family problems should be Sir Michael Egerton and his wife Joanna, the elderly parents of Hereward; and Henry, the self-willed baby of the family. Although the parents recall the elders in *Two Worlds and Their Ways* (1949), Henry is patterned after another Ponsonby, the young Muriel, who in turn, as we have seen, stems from Nevill Sullivan. Henry Egerton contributes little that is essentially new to the type, although his frequent requests to play *Ring-a-rosy* and his trick of pretending to read the Bible (which always

comes out as a rote recitation of nursery rhymes) show a refreshing inventiveness on the author's part.

If the plotting and characterization of *A God and His Gifts*
are on a somewhat reduced scale, the butler Galleon nevertheless receives a bit more attention than other servants in Compton-
Burnett novels of this period. Most important, however, is that
Miss Compton-Burnett's command of mordant, aphoristic wit
in the conversational interchanges remains one of her most brilliant traits.

IX *Conclusion*

These seven novels, as a group, do not surpass the great
achievements of the middle period, the nine novels that begin
with *Men and Wives* and end with *Two Worlds and Their Ways,*
including the criminal works, the "diptych" novels, and the
treatments of children. But, on the other hand, they do not
represent a diminution in power, except in the kitchen comedy,
which continues almost an autonomous and weakened life of
its own, like a branch that is not receiving nourishment from the
main roots. The "diptych" structure in plot continues in the
parallel households of *Darkness and Day, Mother and Son, A
Father and His Fate, A Heritage and Its History,* and *The
Mighty and Their Fall;* the structure is important because it
reflects a balancing of the faults of the one group against those of
the other, which has always been the major moral justification
for this structure. There is also a continuing preoccupation with
illegitimacy and incest as primary plot concerns; *A Father and
His Fate* repeats the success of *Parents and Children* with the
Enoch Arden situation.

The new developments of this period are an increasing austerity in style and in many of the narrative elements. There tend
to be fewer characters than in the early novels with the result
that the family dilemmas have greater concentration and mono-
lithic simplicity. The dialogue tends more toward simplicity and
abstraction, with a moving increase in nobility. Particularly in
Darkness and Day and in *A Heritage and Its History,* the explicit
references to Greek tragedy suggest that this change in dialogue
may be modeled on that source, along with the stichomythia
of *A Father and His Fate.* The achievement of dramatic irony

in the dialogue of *A Heritage and Its History* is indubitably patterned on Greek sources.

Taken on their own merits, with no comparison to preceding novels, these works are an achievement of high consequence; they are full of excitement, somber feelings, and exalted human insights.

CHAPTER 5

Assessments

I English Criticism

THERE is justification in calling Miss Compton-Burnett a novelist's novelist: most of the major critical essays come from writers like Pamela Hansford Johnson, Elizabeth Bowen, P. H. Newby, Kingsley Amis, and Angus Wilson. Robert Liddell, novelist and professor at the University of Cairo, has written the first extended and detailed criticism. Conversely, there are relatively few studies by professional critics and academics.

Miss Hansford Johnson, in surveying the critical reception of Miss Compton-Burnett's work, says that "there can be no doubt that from the publication of *Brothers and Sisters* in 1929 to the present day [1951], Miss Compton-Burnett has been more widely and consistently praised than most writers of her time."[1] She finds that the usual reactions are "enthusiasm, cautious respect, and dispraise" in the proportion of 5:3:2 for *Men and Wives* and 6:1:3 for *More Women than Men*.

Miss Hansford Johnson's pamphlet is a highly creative and imaginative response to the novels, the kind of appreciative criticism in the Pater tradition that is in part a work of art in itself. The richly suggestive style of this pamphlet makes it pleasurable reading; if there is a tendency for the style to carry the meaning away with it, it is an excusable trait in a work that is obviously meant to interest readers in the novels, and one that must still perform that function admirably.

It is, in a sense, a tribute to Miss Hansford Johnson's work that it calls forth discussions on many basic issues of Ivy Compton-Burnett's art which we have touched on elsewhere. She addresses herself particularly to the issue of poetic justice in these novels, concluding with the judgment of amorality that we have already noted. She says that the revolutionary sense of

denouement is especially responsible, calling the ending of *Elders
and Betters* "the most severe shock launched at any reader by
any novelist since the novel first took shape . . ." (13). This is
true in regard to the complete impunity of the evildoer in this
and many another novel. But we must severely qualify the
charge of amorality, for it would seem to imply a complete
failure to distinguish between right and wrong. As we have
noted elsewhere, Miss Compton-Burnett has a very acute moral
sense, and she is entirely on the side of traditional ethical standards. To assert that many evildoers are skillful and wily enough
to get by without punishment is simply an observation of fact,
and one that does not deserve such a sweeping judgment. Any
reader who has once experienced the scene of Charlotte Lamb's
return to her husband must surely be haunted by the ingenuously
simple precision with which Mrs. Lamb tells her husband that
her planned desertion with his cousin Mortimer is a virtuous
act compared to his subtle and unremitting torture of the
children: " 'Mortimer and I did right, not wrong, as you did
always wrong and never right. And now it is clear between us,
and need not be said again.' " And it need not be said again that
this is one of the clearest moral distinctions ever presented in
literature.

In the area of characterization, Miss Hansford Johnson maintains that the personages in these novels are nearly indistinguishable from book to book and that they consist of simple
Dickensian caricatures. As we have seen, Mr. Liddell, among
others, disagrees strongly with this judgment. Actually, there
is reason on both sides; it is largely a question of how much
attention and time the reader wishes to give the works. Recent
studies have revealed that primates maintain a rather complex
social life; the reason we did not know this heretofore is that
we never thought of social life so much as a phenomenon in itself
and we thus lacked the interest to make the observations. In
the same way, careful, interested attention to each nuance of
characterization in these tightly limited novels reveals a rich
variety of differentiated traits among the butlers, fathers, or
elder daughters, each of whom is nevertheless a member of a
general class that reappears again and again.

There seems to be little substance in Miss Hansford Johnson's
assertions about Ivy Compton-Burnett's progressive development

as a novelist, although one must remember that the pamphlet appeared at a time when the author's development was still very much in process. For one thing, the suggestion that Miss Compton-Burnett's visual sense was expanding has not been justified.

By far the most fundamental and authoritative works to date are the third appendix to Robert Liddell's *A Treatise on the Novel* and his book *The Novels of Ivy Compton-Burnett*.[2] The appendix is still the best short discussion of the values of Miss Compton-Burnett's view of the world and of the skills of her art. It is difficult to resist the temptation to quote from it at great length, for it pinpoints the primary qualities of her dialogue, the subtle connections between family tyranny and political Fascism, and the relationship between economic factors and domestic cruelty. Liddell gives a thorough survey of the tyrants who appeared in the novels through *Elders and Betters,* and his summary of the qualities of the good characters is admirable:

Where other novelists are often weak, Miss Compton-Burnett is strong, in the creation of likeable good characters. Her good people are intelligent and nice. They always have those qualities that we really most wish to find in our friends . . . few of the good characters are particularly brave, most of them are irreligious, none of them are at all public-spirited. . . . But they are serious, honest and sensitive, their human values are always right, and they will, if necessary, defend them. They never talk in slang or clichés; they never tell lies to others or to themselves about their feelings or motives . . . while many of the bad characters pride themselves on speaking good of everyone, the good characters know that it may be a higher form of charity to abuse tyrants to their victims, or to allow the victims the rare indulgence of speaking against their tyrants . . . it is by truth, affection and intelligence only that her good characters conquer—and the greatest of these is intelligence. (156)

After a wise treatment of her children and of her general values, Liddell concludes that despite the difficulties of her style, "of all English novelists now writing she is the greatest and the most original artist" (163).

Liddell's book on Ivy Compton-Burnett is frankly polemical, in the best sense of the word: he has obviously been deeply struck by Miss Compton-Burnett as a novelist and he wishes to share his enthusiasm with other readers. This book is designed to be a tribute to her. In a sense it stands beside William Dean Howells's study on Mark Twain, and it ought to be recommended widely as an example of painstaking, thorough, devoted work that shows none of the signs of haste, carelessness, or journalistic superfluity that often characterize early criticism of a living writer.

Liddell's book is also a very personal one, in that he does not shy away from value judgments about human experience, and thus it also avoids the spurious scientistic objectivity of much scholarly writing. Liddell's personal enthusiasm and sympathy for these works is an important factor, because the novels themselves are austere and forbidding enough to discourage many a superficial reader who will not take the trouble to find out what a generously openminded reading can reveal to him. Enumeration and classification are the primary methods of this work; the divisions are "The Tyrants," "The Happenings," "The Victims," "The Chorus," and "The Writing."

Liddell goes to some length to oppose errors in fact or what he finds to be mistaken value judgments in Miss Hansford Johnson's pamphlet; as we have already remarked, he opposes her assertion about the sameness of the characters. In surveying the tyrants, for example, he demonstrates that each one has distinguishable traits that are unique. In addition, he observes that there is a kind of descending order of evil in moving from father tyrants to mothers to aunts, taken as groups. But he also shows that many of the tyrants possess moral probity, generosity, and other creditable traits.

As for the happenings, he does not agree with the frequent charge that the events are insufficiently motivated. He expends much effort to prove, from literary memoirs and famous trials, that the events in themselves not only could have occurred in the actual world but are indeed fairly typical. In other words, he is more concerned with literal, rather than aesthetic, plausibility.

In discussing the victims, Liddell makes the point we have already noted in the criticism of M. Las Vergnas: it is fraternal affection between members of the same generation that is the strongest cohesive emotional force in the novels. The chorus consists of those onlookers who are themselves little concerned with action; these subdivisions are "The Curious," "The Toadies,"

Assessments

"The Prigs," "The Good Governesses," "The Aloof," and "The Lower Orders."

The best part of the chapter on the writing is the discussion of the dialogue; in it Liddell approaches very sensibly some of the issues also raised by Mme. Nathalie Sarraute's essay "Conversation and Sub-Conversation"—that is, the degree to which we can assume that some of the dialogue approaches inaudible personal rumination, or interior monologue. Liddell concludes that we must judge each situation on its own qualities, and that most generalizations will oversimplify the matter. Some of the dialogue is overtly indicated as unspoken, whereas some of it may not have been heard by others. He closes with a discussion of resemblances between some of the passages and the stichomythia of Greek tragedy.

Since Liddell's is a short book of hardly more than one hundred generously spaced pages, it cannot deal in great detail with individual novels. Nor does Liddell attempt to make many comments on progressive developments, such as they are, in Miss Compton-Burnett's writing. In addition, since it was published in 1955, it concerns only the novels through *The Present and the Past*.

A few pages of Arnold Kettle's *An Introduction to the English Novel* are devoted to the analysis of a short passage from *A Family and a Fortune*.[3] Although Kettle recognizes the humanity and decency of Ivy Compton-Burnett's values and the very high quality of her skill, he argues that her willingness to impose rigid limitations in her method constitutes "a retreat that may be tactically discreet but which nevertheless prevents Ivy Compton-Burnett, like Henry Green, from being regarded as a major novelist" (185).

P. H. Newby's pamphlet *The Novel 1945-50* (in the same series as Miss Hansford Johnson's) contains a very short treatment that is remarkable only for one statement, coming as it does from a novelist of considerable stature: "They [the novels] are the only English fiction published since the death of James Joyce about which one can be reasonably sure it will be read a hundred years hence."[4]

Another moving tribute to Miss Compton-Burnett from a working colleague is the essay by Mr. Angus Wilson, the distinguished novelist.[5] Again, as was the case with Liddell, one is tempted to quote at great length because Wilson shows an admirable grasp of exactly what is happening in the novels. He recognizes the firmly traditional elements and the experimental recombinations in the aesthetic sphere; and in the area of values he gives full credit to Miss Compton-Burnett's ethical system and to "her healthy acceptance of life," values to which Louise Bogan and Anthony West have proven themselves curiously blind.

She has explored and made her own the aesthetic ethic, the touch-stone of goodness in taste, decorum and sincerity which was once for all stated by Jane Austen and then miraculously expanded by James and not inconsiderably ornamented by Virginia Woolf and Forster. . . . Finally, it seems to me, that in the total statement of her novels, in what is insufficiently but conveniently described as her "acceptance," she develops straight from the great agnostic artists of the last century. (65)

The paradox at the core of Wilson's very just estimation is that one is repeatedly tempted to classify Miss Compton-Burnett as a "great" novelist, and yet one hesitates to do so before the examples of Jane Austen, Dickens, George Eliot, Tolstoy, and Proust. The only reason for the hesitation is that Miss Compton-Burnett does not demonstrate in her work the deep, unconscious development that characterizes these other novelists.

The manner in which Miss Compton-Burnett so wonderfully suggests real life is, in fact, so similar to that of Tolstoy . . . change and false change, climaxes that are transient, chance remarks that are final, trivialities that take up more attention and energy than death or disaster. It is not that Miss Compton-Burnett is less plumb at the centre of life than her great predecessor, but only that Tolstoy gives us aspects of this centre from a hundred different, revolving mirrors that almost bewilder us by their changing reflections, while she has only one mirror, clear and full, but unchanging. It is, nevertheless, a mirror to be deeply grateful for. (70)

E. D. Pendry's essay in *The New Feminism in English Fiction* constitutes a good introductory discussion of the overall qualities of the works, without any particular attention to individual novels.[6] It contains an especially interesting treatment of the recurrent commonplaces and a thorough discussion of the sense of "anachronism" that sometimes attends the novels. The judgments are sensible and well argued; they are especially valuable in attaining a balanced view of the writer's qualities.

We noted in the discussion of *Mother and Son* the cleanliness of approach to eccentrics like Rosebery Hume and Hester Wolsey. D. W. Jefferson, in "A Note on Ivy Compton-Burnett," makes a similar point in regard to style; he points out that Miss Compton-Burnett inherits from Jane Austen "a tradition of literary and social manners" which holds her subjects at a certain decorous distance, despite "their infirmities beguiling to the modern mind."[7] Thus in dealing with characters whose arrested or fixated sexual development would provide rich material for a psychological case history, Miss Compton-Burnett treats them with a simplicity of diction which is blended with a wittiness that attains true detachment from the subject. Jefferson adds, "The plainness of idiom protects human dignity. So striking is the contrast with modern ways of expression that it is often referred to as 'stylized.' It is a tradition of manners but also one of wit. It would be unprofitable to try to distinguish too closely between the two aspects: between moderation of language as a habit of breeding, and the understatement that operates in the cause of irony" (20-21). Jefferson gives many important additions to E. D. Pendry's discussion of the modernity of approach within a context of Victorian life. His is a short but a very meaty discussion.

Elizabeth Bowen's two perceptive essays on Ivy Compton-Burnett, written for *The New Statesman and Nation* and for *Cornhill Magazine,* have been reprinted in her *Collected Impressions.*[8] In the first essay, she provides a good basic discussion of *Parents and Children,* in the course of which she maintains that Miss Compton-Burnett very rightly relies on the reader's "progressive acquaintanceship" with type-characters in her work, characters who are largely "illustrative" rather than "functional." This distinction we shall reencounter in a slightly different form in the essay by Dr. Lotus Snow.

The second essay, based on *Elders and Betters,* treats Miss Compton-Burnett's work as a continuation of what was left undone by the Victorian novelists; the Edwardians, with their sense of fashionableness and illusion, entirely ignored the un-completed work of their predecessors. "What, then, was this task the Victorians failed to finish, and that the Edwardians declined to regard as theirs? A survey of emotion as an aggressive force, an account of the battle for power that goes on in every unit of English middle-class life" (86). She sees Ivy Compton-Burnett as continuing this tradition from within, stripped of all its inessentials. Elizabeth Bowen finds that the "logic" of Miss Compton-Burnett's development in *Elders and Betters,* as op-posed to *Brothers and Sisters,* consists in a greater closeness to humanity, in the perfection of her melodramatic technique, and in the greater articulateness of the servants.

Given Elizabeth Bowen's admiration for Ivy Compton-Burnett, it seems only just that Edward Sackville-West in his essay "Ladies whose bright Pens . . ." should couple the two novelists.[9] Al-though one may disagree with certain details of his assessment, Sackville-West is a stimulating, urbane writer who stirs up all sorts of curious little insights. He finds that despite the large area of common ground which Miss Compton-Burnett shares with Henry James, she also shows certain similarities to Mrs. Gaskell. But the most brilliant insight in the essay is the parallel he points out with early Cubism:

Like a Picasso of 1913, a Compton-Burnett novel is not concerned with decoration or with observation of the merely contingent, nor is it interested in exhibiting the author's personality or in exploiting a romantic dream. It is constructive, ascetic, low in tone, classical. It enquires into the meanings—the syntactical force—of the things we all say, as the Cubist enquired into the significance of shapes and planes divorced from the incidence of light and the accidents of natural or utilitarian construction. These novels contain very few descriptive passages, and none where description is indulged in for its own sake, or for Impressionistic ends; and in this connection it is significant that Miss Compton-Burnett seems to scorn the aid of images. (86-87)

Sackville-West closes his treatment of Miss Compton-Burnett's "embowered, rook-enchanted concentration camps" with a list of the faults that are frequently found with her work. Neverthe-less, of her total achievement, he finds that the "results are self-evident, timeless, therefore proof against the hysteria of fashion and the blight of political theory" (103).

[114]

II *American Criticism*

The most substantial American recognition has been in Frederick Robert Karl's chapter on Ivy Compton-Burnett in *The Contemporary English Novel.*[10] On the whole, this is a good introductory discussion, but Karl agrees with Pamela Hansford Johnson in assuming that the only morality in the novels is the law of the jungle. That is certainly true of the behavior of two or three of the tyrants; in addition, it is certainly true that in dealing with a raging lion, one would be ill-advised to try rational persuasion, so that the extreme tyrant may inspire jungle-like retaliation from a few of his associates; but this fact hardly justifies the generalization. Karl also finds many of the characters indistinguishable because he feels readers remember particular characters by their predominant emotional responses; he maintains that few of the characters in these novels feel emotion, not even shame or grief. In this assumption, he may also be thinking of the extreme tyrants, but the novels are crowded with very large families, most of whom show abundant capacities for grief and shame, if sometimes in rather convoluted, repressed ways.

These two objections aside, Karl's introductory essay makes good points about the function of the family unit in these novels. In regard to the familiar issue about the degree of "objectivity" to be accorded some of the dialogue, Karl says: "Her conversational method creates, as it were, an external stream of consciousness, in which the characters overtly voice what the traditional novelist usually explains about them" (209).

To this date, the criticism of Miss Compton-Burnett most conspicuously lacks detailed analyses of particular novels, and a rich field is open in this area since each of the works would repay the most minute attention. An excellent beginning has been made by Stanley B. Greenfield in his brilliant piece on *Pastors and Masters.*[11] Greenfield's thesis, which will doubtlessly set a path for much future criticism, leans toward the view that although morality exists, it is largely irrelevant in the power struggle of the tyrant and the victim, which he likens to the Darwinian survival of the fittest. "Yet there is a *necessity* (the word is the author's) in all this; the exploited need their exploiters and are bound to them in many ways. One is reminded

of *The Origin of the Species* [which, it might be added, at least
one of the Compton-Burnett governesses has read] and the
chain of interdependence of species upon species for survival.
In fact, one of the principal movements or patterns in Miss
Compton-Burnett's novels involves a symbiotic relationship in
spite of the victim's efforts to escape the emotional overlordship
imposed upon him into an emotional fulfillment of his own"
(69). He works out his thesis in exhaustive and convincing
detail, showing a richly interlocking series of symmetrical echoes
and parallels. This essay will make a worthy model for future
work on the novels.

The fundamental contribution of Dr. Lotus Snow is in divid-
ing the characters of these novels into two large categories in
relation to two different views of self and of truth to self: "Ivy
Compton-Burnett's leading characters range themselves into
two groups: those who exhibit self by the vehemence of their
acts, and those who reveal self by the penetration of their
speech. The two groups never merge. Those who act never talk
of the motivation of what they do; those who speak freely of
themselves have nothing to conceal."[12]

This distinction, as old as the medieval division into the *vita
activa* and the *vita contemplativa,* also serves to distinguish the
evil from the good to some degree; for, as Dr. Snow indicates,
the latter have nothing to conceal. One wishes she had followed
this point a little further because, as it stands, she insists on the
division a little too heavily. In the novels, there are degrees of
difference between action and contemplation which correspond
somewhat to the degrees of good and evil. But at the extremes,
Dr. Snow is right: "Self—there is no escaping the interpretation—
is the motivation for every human action, and self is greedy for
all the lures of the world, the flesh, and the devil that will
exalt it. The realization offers only one alternative to action:
an intellectual pleasure in observing the machinations of self
in others, a subscription to an orchestra seat at the human
drama" (275-76).

Beekman Waldron Cottrell, in an unpublished dissertation,
has surveyed the modern dialogue novel as practiced by Aldous
Huxley, Henry Green, Ronald Firbank, and Ivy Compton-
Burnett; he finds her aims the broadest and her achievement
the highest of all those who attempt the form.[13] His study is

valuable in pointing out the variety of possibilities in the genre as a whole and in giving a very complete historical context for the dialogue novel.

Cottrell has full and interesting analyses of typical children and servants in these novels. Like Dr. Snow, Cottrell attempts to find figurative significance in Miss Compton-Burnett's distinctive names. While it is obvious that some names come from Shakespeare, and many from literature (Herrick, Donne, Swift, Bacon), these must simply be taken as *jeux d'esprit*. Miss Compton-Burnett is one of the most dryly unmetaphorical of writers, and any attempt to relate a character named "Duncan" to the basic problems of *Macbeth* invariably distorts her aims. For what it is worth, Miss Compton-Burnett, in a letter to the author, disavows any symbolic significance in the names.

Of all the general introductions, that of Bernard McCabe, "Ivy Compton-Burnett, An English Eccentric," is one of the most complete; he includes in his essay more comment on her general development than is usual, along with the customary discussion of the author's own peculiar conventions.[14] The most valuable feature of the essay is his judicious assessment of the broadest aspects of Miss Compton-Burnett's values. In the inevitable comparison with Jane Austen, he finds that Miss Compton-Burnett shows a "knowingness" rather than the "wisdom" we find in her predecessor, a "clever, rapid, ironic, pinpointing" understanding that is too cerebral for complete moral awareness; it is easy to imagine that the less cerebral qualities that would complete her vision are the very factors that Angus Wilson also found lacking in the failure of what he called "unconscious development."

McCabe feels that when a final crisis forces them to the wall, all of her characters—persecutors and persecuted—resort to an assertion of individual independence: "their right to exist as they are, without in the end any obligation to anyone but themselves." This ultimate, ironic repudiation of authority is "complementary to a deterministic resignation . . . and it is the reiteration of these two attitudes, and her evident attachment to them that more than anything else suggests an essential immaturity and consequent limitation in Miss Compton-Burnett's approach to moral situations" (63).

In an unpublished master's thesis, "An Analytical Study of

Children in the Novels of I. Compton-Burnett," Vera P. Krieger makes a careful study of the types of child characters. She discusses their relative importance in relation to themes and plots, putting welcome emphasis on the children's consciousness of the necessity to play roles in order to please their elders.[15] Miss Krieger rejects Miss Hansford Johnson's idea that the children constitute a hopeful element in the novels; she finds that the children's victories are largely pyrrhic and temporary. The implication is that they are not going to reform the world they were born into—they will simply learn to live in it.

III *French Criticism*

At least five of Miss Compton-Burnett's novels have been translated into French;[16] Cecily Mackworth, in surveying these translations, indicates that the novels have not won a large reading public in France because of their lack of an obvious surface appeal and because of their austere texture. There are also great difficulties in translating dialogue so that it carries the subtle nuances which the English reader absorbs almost without thought. Nevertheless, Miss Mackworth finds parallels between these novels and the works of the school of young contemporary French novelists—Nathalie Sarraute, Michel Butor, and Alain Robbe-Grillet. Miss Mackworth's case is convincing to the extent that Ivy Compton-Burnett shows a similar intensity of purpose and economy of means which dispense with all the comfortable novelistic padding that has been sanctified by tradition. As far as the male novelists are concerned, Miss Mackworth says they are as devoted to "objects" as Miss Compton-Burnett is to "sound," a parallel that is somewhat tenuous.

There is a comparatively substantial body of introductory essays on Ivy Compton-Burnett's novels in French journals; by far the most interesting of these is that of Nathalie Sarraute. This distinguished pioneer in the so-called "anti-novel" school of writers praises Miss Compton-Burnett as "one of the greatest novelists that England has ever had."[17] While much of her essay "Conversation and Sub-Conversation" sounds like the strong literary polemic of a new school eager to establish its own pantheon, these remain words of glowing tribute.

Mme. Sarraute announces in her essay "The Age of Suspicion"

that a mutual suspicion plagues both readers and writers in our day. The outmoded conventions of character and plot are as repellent to present needs as were the outworn techniques of perspective discarded by painters in this century. The true business of the contemporary novelist—for her—is in the evocation of infinitely subtle psychological states common to all experience, and thus the novelist's real aim is only partially relevant to old-fashioned devices of plotting and characterization. In this essay, she recommends the "anonymous I" as a nameless narrative consciousness.

In "Conversation and Sub-Conversation," the same hostility to the outworn "behaviorist novel" and to the interior monologue of the James Joyce–Virginia Woolf epoch draws Mme. Sarraute's attention to Henry Green and to Ivy Compton-Burnett for their heavy reliance on dialogue. In praising their efforts, she welcomes a reliance on words rather than actions as the medium of revealing subtle interior movements of the psyche and their random, seemingly innocuous eruption into the glaring light of exterior reality. In his preface to Mme. Sarraute's novel *Portrait of a Man Unknown,* Jean-Paul Sartre reinforces this point by suggesting that the whole distinction between subjective and objective is a false one.[18] He defines the essential aim of her form as putting into play subjectivity and objectivity, generalization and particularization, the authentic and the inauthentic. By moving from one pole to the other, she catches the elusive reality which is sure to be lost if a writer espouses any one of these qualities to the exclusion of its opposite.

These points are germane to any discussion of Miss Compton-Burnett. Mme. Sarraute certainly respects her English predecessor for breaking ground, for showing how dialogue can serve expressive functions never heretofore conceived of.

To pursue the question of Miss Compton-Burnett's possible influence on Mme. Sarraute may be futile, since Miss Compton-Burnett has indicated in correspondence that she and Mme. Sarraute are agreed that there is no mutual influence. In the same letter she indicates that she is not acquainted with Mme. Sarraute's work in detail. Let us therefore see what resemblances exist between their works.

In Mme. Sarraute's novels, the break with Joyce, Woolf, Proust, and Gide is not so complete as we might expect. If we take *Portrait of a Man Unknown* as an example, we have the familiar nervously sensitive first-person narrator, a man who is under psychiatric care for extreme introversion. He is obsessed by the attempt to discover the real nature of an elderly miser and his daughter. The book is very unlike the typical Compton-Burnett approach in that it is plotless, it involves relatively little dialogue in the conventional sense, and the style burgeons with poetic metaphor. In addition, there are no traces of comedy.

But these differences do not end the matter, for in the content and the emotional response to it, we find in the father's tyrannical hold over his daughter—and in her symbiotic need of him—echoes of a situation dear to the heart of Miss Compton-Burnett. However, as one of the characters of the novel remarks, the situation might have come with equal ease out of Julien Green or François Mauriac—the phrase "nest of vipers" occurring in the text.

Mme. Sarraute's unnamed tyrant nevertheless strikingly recalls, among other Compton-Burnett tyrants, Horace Lamb of *Bullivant and the Lambs,* particularly in his avarice. If Horace had met his French counterpart, he might have learned a few more tricks, such as having the children wear black underclothes to simplify laundry problems. The tension that distorts and debases the lives of the father and the daughter is a French *petit-bourgeois* version of the same intense, puritanical earnestness that motivates Harriet Haslam and Andrew Stace. In the supremely painful interview in which the father argues about his daughter's medical expenses, the narrator indicates that the one word which it would be impossible to use in the presence of this spitting pair is *désinvolture*—ease, freedom, familiarity of intercourse.

But the fundamental value that Miss Compton-Burnett's artistic example may have for Mme. Sarraute is not to be found in the obvious, gross distinctions of style, structure, or content. It is most decidedly in the use of dialogue as an illustration of how conventional means can be adapted to unconventional ends that Miss Compton-Burnett, and to a lesser degree Henry Green, stimulate Mme. Sarraute's admiration. On this matter, Mme. Sarraute says:

These long, stilted sentences, which are at once stiff and sinuous, do not recall any conversations we ever heard. And yet, although they seem strange, they never give an impression of being spurious or gratuitous.

The reason for this is that they are located not in an imaginary place, but in a place that actually exists: somewhere on the fluctuating frontier that separates conversation from sub-conversation. Here the inner movements, of which the dialogue is merely the outcome and, as it were, the furthermost point—usually prudently tipped to allow it to come up to the surface—try to extend their action into the dialogue itself. To resist their constant pressure and contain them, the conversation stiffens, becomes stilted, it adopts a cautious, slackened pace. But it is because of this pressure that it stretches and twists into long sinuous sentences. Now a close, subtle game, which is also a savage game, takes place between the conversation and the sub-conversation. ("Conversation," 114)

It would be a mistake, of course, to read too much subjectivity into Miss Compton-Burnett's method; Mme. Sarraute protects herself against this misunderstanding thus:

No doubt this method is content to make the reader constantly suspect the existence, the complexity and the variety of the inner movements. It does not make him acquainted with them, in the way that techniques which plunged him into their depths and made him navigate through their currents, could succeed in doing. But it has at least the superiority over these latter techniques of having immediately attained to perfection. And by so doing it has succeeded in giving to traditional dialogue the worst blow it has received so far. ("Conversation," 116)

Obviously this "bad blow" that Miss Compton-Burnett struck was the use of dialogue for all expressive functions in the novel. Heretofore, each expressive function in the traditional novel had its fixed vehicle or medium of communication. Dialogue was enclosed in straight-jacketed quotation marks (even more constraining in traditional French punctuation), with rigid conventions of the "he expostulated," "she responded" variety. Also, it was decreed that dialogue be used exclusively for articulated speech; characterization, setting, development, reverie—each had its formally decreed vehicle of expression. Miss Compton-Burnett, by contrast, took one of the vehicles alone—dialogue—and used it for all the expressive functions; this was an audacious readjustment of vehicle to function.

Now we have seen that Mme. Sarraute is not interested in the dialogue novel *per se* as a means of expression, since she uses less dialogue than many another novelist. What excited her was this audacity in breaking down the boundaries between the decreed expressive function and the decreed vehicles of communication. In her own work the result can be seen most clearly in the climactic scene to which we have already referred —the interview about the daughter's medical expenses in *Portrait of a Man Unknown*. Here we find the wavering line between dialogue and exposition and poetic reverie, without a strictly formal use of quotation marks; all vehicles function together for all purposes and the result is—as various leading French critics have said—that Mme. Sarraute is expressing something entirely new in the novel. Moreover, there is no fixed point of view, even though most of the novel has been managed through a narrator; and it may also be to Miss Compton-Burnett's abolishment of a fixed point of view through dialogue that we owe another part of Mme. Sarraute's achievement.

Mme. Sarraute, who reads the Compton-Burnett novels in English, must have a lively sense of connotative nuances. We have seen that Ivy Compton-Burnett makes a masterful use of cliché, platitude, truism, and folk-saying for a variety of purposes. Mme. Sarraute is equally accomplished at this kind of stylistic distinction, but she exalts the cliché to a grandly philosophical and symbolic level, amply indicated by Jean-Paul Sartre's discussion of her technique in his preface to *Portrait*. In the fierce hostility to the "inauthentic" bourgeois evasions, the sensitive narrator is pained and fascinated by the use of the cliché on the part of "them," the unnamed father and daughter. It is one of their ruses to clothe their inner terrors and uncertainties; it is their carapace, their shell that protects them from reality. In the insistent insect and undersea imagery of this novel, the tendrils, tentacles, and antennae symbolize the "interior movements," whereas the shell and carapace stand for bourgeois cliché. The daughter is supported in her clichés by a chorus of elderly, proper, gloved ladies; and the father is equally sustained by a corresponding group of hardheaded businessmen. While Miss Compton-Burnett uses the cliché baldly and is as often as not on the side of the platitudinous person, Mme. Sarraute imbues the cliché with much stronger emotional connotations.

Thus we can see that Mme. Sarraute is a distinctly original novelist whose debt to Miss Compton-Burnett cannot be gauged in obvious terms; but, on the other hand, it is difficult to conceive of what her art would have been without Miss Compton-Burnett's example.

Other French notices have, on the whole, dealt generously and understandingly with Miss Compton-Burnett's work. Miss Mackworth, whom we have already mentioned, shows beautiful insight into the workings of falsehood in these novels and how falsehood is related to the lifeblood of tyranny. It is disappointing, however, that she fails to see Miss Compton-Burnett's basic respect for stability:

> Because the pessimism of this author supposes that order does not exist. As for the lie, it is there in order to permit continued existence to those who do not have enough strength or grandeur of soul to sustain such a harsh reality. Deliberate lies, by which persons seek to impose on others; lies in their very natures, by which they seek to deceive themselves; even more profound lies by which they seek to create an illusory order . . . all aim at hiding or denying this terrible and essential absence. ("Les Romans d'Ivy Compton-Burnett," 339)

Like Robert Liddell, she distinguishes between the tyranny of Theobald Pontifex in *The Way of All Flesh* and that of the Compton-Burnett variety: "With her, tyranny reveals itself as an intrinsic element of the human condition rather than as a flaw that could be eliminated. Its absence would not reestablish any harmony whatsoever, because in disappearing it would destroy the very matter—made of an inextricable network of good and evil—of man's psychology" ("Les Romans," 402). Miss Mackworth comes very close to confirming the view, given earlier in this volume, that manners are of high importance in the Compton-Burnett novel, even in crime: "People will kill, but there will never be any blood; they will push others to suicide, but not one indecorous word will be pronounced. Tyranny is envisaged as a state of fact, carrying with it certain consequences which will surprise no one" ("Les Romans," 403).

Maurice Cranston, an English critic writing for a French review, gives an admirably simple general introduction to Miss Compton-

Burnett's works. When he discusses her value system, he makes her sound, curiously enough, like another Tennessee Williams: "In the novels of Miss Compton-Burnett, it is weakness and not wickedness that is punished, because it is weakness, as she conceives it, which is punished in life" ("Ivy Compton-Burnett," 430). But the difference we might expect between Mr. Williams's view of the weak person overwhelmed by the stronger and that of Miss Compton-Burnett is given thus: "Miss Compton-Burnett shows herself full of compassion toward those who suffer, toward the victims of evil. But she is a fatalist, she does not see what one could do to change the face of things. The weak succumb and that is that. What must happen, happens, and no one loses any time crying over what could not be other than it is" (433). Cranston concludes with a judgment that echoes the remarks of many a character in the novels: "What is essential to us in these books is the feeling that the most frightful sins—murder, incest, etc.—cause infinitely fewer ravages than the continual wickednesses, disputes, vexations, and cantankerousness with which the web of bourgeois life is woven" (439).

Most of the information in Raymond Las Vergnas' article on Miss Compton-Burnett appears to come directly out of Robert Liddell's study, and it provides very little to the specialized reader except for one or two interesting insights about the nature of love and about the character of the "hero" in these novels.[19] M. Las Vergnas indicates that romantic attitudes, be they rose colored or black, have no place here. The strongest cohesion between persons is fraternal affection, which unites the victims of tyranny in a universe that would be otherwise insupportable. "But appearing almost involuntarily through the cascade of witty words, a great affirmation of human solidarity rises like a rock. This feeling, this sharp consciousness of community, paradoxically explains the apparent coldness of tone. A coldness at the same time cause and consequence of the author's refusal to judge" (119). Although he must conceive of the word in a rather special context, M. Las Vergnas treats the Ivy Compton-Burnett "hero" as if he were directly within the tradition of English empirical hedonism:

The integral doubt which the author demonstrates is equivalent to a lucid wisdom based on disenchantment. The hero is he who, having established an Epicurean harmony in terms of his tastes, peacefully follows the course of his destiny. He, on the contrary, who deliberately sacrifices himself to others can expect no recompense. His deception, moreover, would be merited. The mutilation which he imposes on himself is absurd. The fundamental crime is the sin against intelligence (*l'esprit*): stupidity. The rest is but a passing convulsion which inscribes itself on the thread of days without altering the web." (119-20)

IV The Opposition

Those critics who are hostile to Miss Compton-Burnett are easily classified in one sense, but difficult to define in detail. They cannot read her books sympathetically because their political, social, and aesthetic assumptions are antithetical to the "aesthetic ethic" which Angus Wilson discussed. Perhaps the best introduction to their attitude is provided by Kenneth Allsop in some opening remarks from his book *The Angry Decade*, in which he specifies his reasons for not treating Miss Compton-Burnett, among many others:

Rather like the American Republicans who, Adlai Stevenson once said, had been "dragged kicking and screaming into the Twentieth Century," the survivors of the old *literati*, the candelabra-and-wine *rentier* writers have taken the Fifties on sufferance. Wincing with distaste, mournful and puzzled, they have withdrawn to a remote and musty fantasy life among their woodland temples. Their considerable talent is absorbed into the construction of elaborate, private languages, elegiac remembrance of things past, reveries that are passed like an empty parcel around an ever diminishing circle. Their writing becomes more and more heavily wrought with convoluted scroll-work, or more and more allusive, quivering with *nuance,* gauzy with conversational subtleties that taper off into the raising of an eyebrow.[20]

Although it is difficult to argue against clever writing, the most substantial charge made here is that of fantasy, a charge that occurs frequently among critics of this orientation. At the outset it must be recognized that "fantasy" is not a dirty word; it simply describes a literary genre which suspends the laws of cause and effect in order to deal with the wonderful, the childlike, and the improbable. At a deeper level, it could be argued that any fantasy is simply an elaborate metaphor. Thus the charge sounds strange, coming from the pen of such an adept user of metaphor. But more importantly, Miss Compton-

Burnett's books are not fantasies. Despite their nineteenth-century country milieu, their remoteness from ordinary speech, and their lack of realistic detail, they concern the most vital moral issues of individual experience within the family context. They occur in distant times because they concern universal human problems of all times, and they are more easily objectified by the remoteness of the setting. The kind of art that Allsop and his colleagues call for is far more open to the charge of irrelevancy; for, under the specious urgency of treating important current issues in public life, this superficial journalistic art loses all touch with what is fundamentally important and enduring in human experience.

Kenneth Allsop's points are given a fuller and more detailed expression by Kingsley Amis, who is himself a figurehead for a very realistic school of writing.[21] Amis makes the familiar charges that Miss Compton-Burnett's characters are not sufficiently delineated, that the plots are melodramatic and arbitrary, that the dialogue is artificial, and that the world represented in these novels is impervious to progress, change, or development. He differs from many other critics in that he supports these objections by a rather detailed discussion that amounts to a critique of Miss Compton-Burnett's aesthetic. His objections have their own kind of validity for someone who is irritated by not having felt the justification for these mannerisms.

In many cases, however, the objections result from a lack of sympathy that blinds him to the fact that Miss Compton-Burnett is often doing quite the same thing that he asks for, but in the only way possible to her. He says, for example, that what the characters say is not so striking as the number of things one could not conceive of their saying. "To imagine what would have to happen before a Compton-Burnett character could say 'You bore me' or 'What a pretty dress' or 'Give me a kiss' or 'Oh my God' is an instructive experience" (173). Amis could spare himself this exercise of imagination if he could see how palpably Camilla Bellamy tells her estranged rector-husband in Chapter V of *Men and Wives* of the boredom of his way of life:

"I have had my fill of funerals, and mothers' meetings and parishioners' teas. The funerals are the best; they do get rid of somebody. We emerge from them with one parishioner less. They are better than the weddings, which promise us a further supply. Funerals have never failed us. Your flock behave at last with a decent self-efface-ment. The drawback is that they give you the opportunity of doing the opposite. I couldn't cloud my last days as your wife with the spectacle of your doing yourself justice at a funeral." (*Men*, 49-50)

As for the "What a pretty dress" variety, Amis can find copious examples in *More Women than Men, Two Worlds and Their Ways*, and *Daughters and Sons*; but, if he means by this kind of speech the vacuous social amenity of the Dale Carnegie variety, he will be disappointed.

The problem Amis raises of the lack of change in these novels is a thorny one. No one denies that these are the sort of books in which a husband and wife discover, after the birth of three children, that they are half brother and sister; here is a sudden enough change in their lives. But Amis's argument is that the development is too sudden and arbitrary and that it does not lead to any change in the attitudes of the characters. Karl made a similar point in objecting that the "recognition scenes" in these novels do not stimulate the characters toward moral regeneration, as we must assume Oedipus's "recognition" did.

The only answer to be made to this objection is that change *can* occur, as in Horace Lamb's determination to rectify his tyrannical ways after his wife nearly runs off with his cousin —or when Simon Challoner shows an almost total change of character after he finally inherits his estate. But the change in Horace is not a permanent one, and we see him reverting to his old ways in the last scene of the novel. This kind of change turns into the habitual, self-seeking "moral regeneration" of the camp-meeting variety, so acutely demonstrated in the case of Huckleberry Finn's drunkard father. Miss Compton-Burnett herself obliquely comments on Oedipus's regeneration in *Dark-ness and Day* where she says that his change may have done good to him, but that to his daughter it meant complete servitude to a blind old man. In his daughter's eyes, Oedipus's change of attitude could hardly be seen except as arrant selfishness, since she had to lead him around from city to city on his moral mis-sion. Thus what appears to be change is often the recrudescence of the same old evil in a new form: *plus ça change, plus c'est la même chose*. To the Classical and Neoclassical artist, stability is a precious value because it is inherently characteristic of the universe as he sees it.

We must take these critics' word for their dissatisfaction with the lack of change; but we must also point out that Miss Compton-Burnett has every right to see the world as she sees it and to represent it truly. Many leftist critics attempted to take Hemingway to task for his failure of social consciousness in novels like *A Farewell to Arms,* but they should have been chastened by *To Have and Have Not,* which shows what a bad book can be produced if the author tries to force his talent into uncongenial channels.

Bewilderingly enough, those critics who are sympathetic with Miss Compton-Burnett's work sometimes make quite the opposite assertion—that the sudden changes prove her to be a complete relativist for whom value does not exist except within specific contexts. Angus Wilson, in fact, argues that Miss Compton-Burnett uses incest and illegitimacy as plot devices in the same way that Shakespeare does in his comedies: to undermine any concepts of stability of personality. This is also, essentially, the thesis of Cecily Mackworth.

To return to Amis's assessment, he concludes that Miss Compton-Burnett is saved by her sense of the comic, which is a valuable comment since he is primarily known as a comic novelist himself. On the serious side he admires her hatred for tyranny and her pity for the victim. Even though he has accused her of "triviality" and "fantasy," he concludes that she is "our most original living novelist."

Among American critics, Orville Prescott and Anthony West show the same tendency as Kenneth Allsop in couching their attacks in brilliantly corrosive philippic.[22] West lumps Miss Compton-Burnett's novels together with those of Henry James in the category of escapist historical fiction, pretty and innocuous daydreams. His brilliantly prejudiced assessment is the definitive word for those readers who are irrationally predisposed to scoff at "afternoon tea letters."

Thus the criticism of Miss Compton-Burnett is in general overly strong in general studies that catalog the eccentricities and idiosyncrasies of her method, but it is unnecessarily weak in detailed studies of particular novels. The one error common to the largest number of the critics is the rather hasty assumption that, because the author has the honesty to say that man can and does perform gross evil with impunity, her world lacks moral distinctions. On the contrary, there is a very rigid system of standards implicit in the novels, based on empirical human invention; the horror at the core of these books is that the awesome female tyrants hold themselves above compliance with the standards; but, without the violation of standards, there would be no drama. The fact that the system can prolong its validity in the face of such unscrupulous creatures is the test that proves its rightness. Even Greenfield, who has contributed the most brilliant (and the only) detailed analysis of the operation of the system, falls into the "law of the jungle" fallacy to some degree. The symbiotic relationship which he finds in *Pastors and Masters* represents the eternal interdependence of good and evil that is the theme of all profound literary creation. But without the ultimate hope that the struggle is worth carrying forward, there would be no point in writing books.

V   *Conclusion*

The dialogue novels of Ivy Compton-Burnett are works of high literacy and intelligence that are in the mainstream of an English literary tradition that runs from Jane Austen through the Brontës, for they combine a depiction of the most mannered civilization with the Gothic horrors of incest and infanticide. Their technique is sparse, austere, and dry, with absolutely no concessions to popular taste. Their major concerns run tangentially against the bias of our age. Aside from the precocious and articulate children, they represent the experience of a rural gentry in late middle age and in extreme old age, for whom the passions of the flesh are persistent ghosts of past mistakes that haunt their peace. Economically insecure, agnostic, committed to a family life which is as exacerbating as it is inevitable, these gentlefolk pass leisured mornings and afternoons largely in protracted conversations about their lot.

The secondary tensions of these novels are in emotional attachments between unmarried persons and between mother and son, father and daughter, brother and sister, man and man, and woman and woman; the countertensions are the proprieties of a tradition that enforces taboos against these alliances. The stability of the society lies in the control of family authority. But where there are control and authority, there is power; and thus the primary tensions are those involved in the seeking, gaining, holding, and enforcing of this power. The basic Latin stem for "authority" is a verb meaning "to produce, to increase," and thus in a dynastic context the authority is rightly granted to the oldest living person who has produced or increased off-spring in the sanctioned connubial relationship. But by this very productiveness, the authority figure has given rise to a large group of persons who, given the limits of primogeniture, cannot themselves occupy positions of authority; and they are thus thrown back on the secondary adulterous, incestuous, and monosexual outlets which in turn must be controlled.

The rhythmic interplay between those in power and those out of power has as its fugal accompaniment the tensions of those in the sanctioned connubial relationship against those in taboo relationships. This central paradox, which is the real subject of the novels, is brilliantly stated toward the end of *Two Worlds and Their Ways:*

"We can only hide our heads at home. Homes cause the shame, but they also provide a hiding-place for it, and we have to take one thing with another."

"You would hardly think homes would be so fair," said Clemence.

At a lower level of "subject matter," the course of Miss Compton-Burnett's development is clear. The first three novels —*Dolores, Pastors and Masters,* and *Brothers and Sisters*—are exploratory ones in which technique is consolidated; the follow-ing "criminal triad"—*Men and Wives, More Women than Men,* and *A House and Its Head*—deal with situations involving mur-der. The next six works—*Daughters and Sons, A Family and a Fortune, Parents and Children, Elders and Betters, Bullivant and the Lambs,* and *Two Worlds and Their Ways*—which are among her greatest novels, are characterized by a detailed ex-ploration of childhood and the inclusion of servant life; accom-panying these developments are the masterful employment of the "diptych" technique for balancing parallel groups and com-pensatory moral "stumbles." The final seven novels—*Darkness and Day, The Present and the Past, Mother and Son, A Father and His Fate, A Heritage and Its History, The Mighty and Their*

Assessments

Fall, and *A God and His Gifts*—continue to treat of incest, divorce, remarriage, and inheritance; they show greater simplicity, austerity, and nobility than their predecessors. All the works are characterized by a homogenous blending of tragedy and comedy within the dialogue convention.

In her originality and in her uncompromising honesty to her own inspiration, Miss Compton-Burnett is the unchallenged master of the current English novel. She is herself as removed from the ephemeral literary preoccupations of her day as the Gothic sculpture on a cathedral overlooking a busy thoroughfare. While this remoteness can be confused with imperviousness to time, P. H. Newby's assertion that she is the only writer since Joyce who is likely to be read one hundred years from now is as safe a statement as any contemporary could risk.

Notes and References

Chapter One

1. Stanley J. Kunitz, ed., *Twentieth Century Authors*, First Supplement (New York, 1955), p. 222.
2. W. J. Weatherby, "Tea at Four," *Manchester Guardian*, Air Mail Edition, LXXXVI (May 17, 1962), p. 11.
3. Established by a manufacturer of patent medicine as a private college in 1883 and opened by Queen Victoria in 1886, Royal Holloway College, Englefield Green, Surrey, was admitted to the Faculty of Arts and Sciences of the University of London in 1899. Its aim was "to afford the best education for women of the middle and upper classes. . . . The College shall neither be considered or conducted as a mere training college for teachers and governesses." R. J. S. McDowall and D. M. Gurney, *The Story of the University of London* (London, 1952), p. 16.
4. Letter from Dr. Batho, June 27, 1962. The set books studied in her first year are as follows: Virgil, *Georgics*, I and IV; Tacitus, *Germania*; Sophocles, *Ajax*; Plato, *Menexenus*. In the following two years she probably read these Pass course books: Cicero, *De Oratore*, I and *Pro Milone*; Plautus, *Trinummus*; Lucretius, Book V; Sophocles, *Oedipus Rex*; Demosthenes, *De Corona*; Homer, *Odyssey*, IX, XI, XII; Plato, *Gorgias*. In addition, she would have read these Honors course books: Tacitus, *Annals*, I; Horace, *Epistles* and *Ars Poetica*; Aristophanes, *The Knights*; and Thucydides, Book IV. And for 1907: Cicero, *Ad Atticum*, II; Virgil, *Ecologues*; Herodotus, Book II; and Sophocles, *Philoctetes*. In all this, as Dr. Batho points out, Aristotle is conspicuously absent.
5. *The Mighty and Their Fall* (New York, 1962), p. 88.
6. *Mother and Son* (New York, 1955), p. 44.
7. *A Family and a Fortune* (London, 1949), p. 259.
8. *Parents and Children* (London, 1947), p. 112.
9. *A Father and His Fate* (New York, 1958), p. 79.
10. *Darkness and Day* (New York, 1951), pp. 240-41.
11. *A House and Its Head* (London, 1935), p. 78.
12. *Daughters and Sons* (London, 1950), pp. 290-91.

Notes and References

13. *Men and Wives* (London, 1948), p. 69.
14. "A Conversation Between I. Compton-Burnett and M. Jourdain," in *Orion, A Miscellany* (London, 1945), p. 25.

Chapter Two

1. Letter from Miss Compton-Burnett, August 7, 1962.
2. Letter from Dr. Batho, June 27, 1962. "They were all persons of high scholarship and marked individuality, and it is amusing to find their shadows in this novel speaking in the accents with which we are familiar in Miss Compton-Burnett's other books, but this may not be surprising, as she was not herself a member of the Senior (i.e. Faculty) Common Room and relied on guesswork when her characters are not speaking to students."
3. Letter from Miss Compton-Burnett, August 7, 1962.
4. *Pastors and Masters* (London, 1952), pp. 111-12.
5. *Brothers and Sisters* (London, 1954), pp. 100-01.

Chapter Three

1. *Elders and Betters* (London, 1952), p. 37.
2. *I. Compton-Burnett*, Bibliographical Series of Supplements to British Book News (London, 1951), p. 11.
3. *Bullivant and the Lambs* (New York, 1948), p. 144.
4. Letter from Miss Compton-Burnett, July, 1962.
5. *Two Worlds and Their Ways* (New York, 1949), p. 291.

Chapter Four

1. *A Heritage and Its History* (New York, 1960), p. 117.

Chapter Five

1. *I. Compton-Burnett*, Biographical Series of Supplements to British Book News, p. 37.
2. *A Treatise on the Novel* (London, 1947), Appendix III, pp. 146-63; *The Novels of I. Compton-Burnett* (London, 1955).
3. *An Introduction to the English Novel* (New York, 1960), Vol. II, pp. 184-90.
4. *I. Compton-Burnett*, Bibliographical Series of Supplements to British Book News, p. 31.
5. "Ivy Compton-Burnett," *The London Magazine*, II (July, 1955), 64-70.

6. *The New Feminism in English Fiction* (Tokyo, 1956), pp. 90-119.

7. *A Review of English Literature*, I (April, 1960), 19-24.

8. (London, New York, and Toronto, 1950), pp. 82-91.

9. *Inclinations* (London, 1949), pp. 78-103.

10. (New York, 1962), pp. 201-19.

11. "'Pastors and Masters': The Spoils of Genius," *Criticism*, II (Winter, 1960), 66-80.

12. "'Good is Bad Condensed': Ivy Compton-Burnett's View of Human Nature," *Western Humanities Review*, X (Summer, 1956), 273.

13. "Conversation Piece: Four Twentieth-Century English Dialogue Novelists," unpublished dissertation, Columbia University, 1956.

14. *Critique*, III (Winter-Spring, 1960), 47-63.

15. Unpublished master's thesis, Bowling Green State University, 1964.

16. Robert Vidal has translated *Les Ponsonby* (*Daughters and Sons*) 1947; *Les Vertueux Aînés* (*Elders and Betters*) 1950; *Une Famille et Son Chef* (*A House and Its Head*) 1954; and *Des Hommes et des Femmes* (*Men and Wives*) 1958; these are all Gallimard editions.

Ludmilla Stavitzki translated *Plus de Femmes que d'Hommes* (*More Women Than Men*) for Editions du Seuil in 1950. See Cecily Mackworth, "Les Romans d'Ivy Compton-Burnett," *Critique* (Paris), XIV (May, 1958), 396-404; and Maurice Cranston, "Ivy Compton-Burnett," tr. Renée Villoteau, *Lettres Nouvelles*, No. 64, 425-40. I am responsible for the translation of all quotations in this section except for those from Mme. Sarraute.

17. "Conversation and Sub-Conversation," *The Age of Suspicion*, tr. Maria Jolas (New York, 1963), p. 112.

18. *Portrait d'un Inconnu* (Paris, 1956). This novel has been translated by Maria Jolas as *Portrait of a Man Unknown* (New York, 1958).

19. "Ivy Compton-Burnett," *La Revue de Paris*, LXVIII (September, 1960), 114-21.

20. (London, 1958), pp. 24-25.

21. "One World and Its Way," *The Twentieth Century*, CLVIII (August, 1955), 168-75.

22. Orville Prescott, "Comrades of the Coterie," *In My Opinion* (Indianapolis and New York, 1952), pp. 92-109; Anthony West, "Ivy Compton-Burnett," *Principles and Persuasions* (New York, 1957), pp. 225-32.

Selected Bibliography

PRIMARY SOURCES

Brothers and Sisters. London: Victor Gollancz, 1954.
Bullivant and the Lambs. New York: Alfred A. Knopf, 1948.
Darkness and Day. New York: Alfred A. Knopf, 1951.
Daughters and Sons. London: Victor Gollancz, 1950.
Dolores. London: Wm. Blackstone & Son, 1911.
Elders and Betters. London: Victor Gollancz, 1952.
A Family and a Fortune. London: Eyre and Spottiswoode, 1949.
A Father and His Fate. New York: Julian Messner, 1958.
A God and His Gifts. New York: Simon and Schuster, 1964.
A Heritage and Its History. New York: Simon and Schuster, 1960.
A House and Its Head. London: William Heinemann, Ltd., 1935.
Men and Wives. London: Eyre and Spottiswoode, 1948.
The Mighty and Their Fall. New York: Simon and Schuster, 1962.
More Women than Men. London: William Heinemann, Ltd., 1933.
Mother and Son. New York: Julian Messner, 1955.
Parents and Children. London: Victor Gollancz, 1947.
Pastors and Masters. London: Victor Gollancz, 1952.
The Present and the Past. New York: Julian Messner, 1953.
Two Worlds and Their Ways. New York: Alfred A. Knopf, 1949.

SECONDARY SOURCES

Allsop, Kenneth. *The Angry Decade.* London: Peter Owen, 1958.
    Contains a general attack on writers of Miss Compton-Burnett's
    orientation.
Amis, Kingsley. "One World and Its Way," *The Twentieth Century,*
    CLVIII (August, 1955), 168-75. A perspicacious analysis by a
    largely unsympathetic fellow novelist which represents the most
    reasoned statement of the Realists' case against Miss Compton-
    Burnett's art.
Bowen, Elizabeth. *Collected Impressions.* New York: Longmans,
    Green, 1950. Penetrating and admiring remarks on *Parents and
    Children* and *Elders and Betters* by a distinguished colleague.
"A Conversation Between I. Compton-Burnett and M. Jourdain,"
    Orion, A Miscellany, Vol. I. London: Nicholson and Watson,

1945. A very thorough discussion of the author's art between Miss Compton-Burnett and her lifelong companion; this document is as close to an artistic credo as the novelist has ever produced.

Cottrell, Beekman Waldron. "Conversation Piece: Four Twentieth-Century English Dialogue Novelists." Unpublished dissertation, Columbia University, 1956. A historical discussion of the dialogue novel and a comparison of the art of Aldous Huxley, Henry Green, Ronald Firbank and Ivy Compton-Burnett.

Cranston, Maurice. "Ivy Compton-Burnett," tr. Renée Villoteau, *Lettres Nouvelles*, No. 64, 425-40. A good general introduction in French.

Greenfield, Stanley B. " 'Pastors and Masters': The Spoils of Genius," *Criticism*, II (Winter, 1960), 68-80. A very detailed analysis of the author's first distinctive novel and one of the finest pieces in all Compton-Burnett criticism.

Jefferson, D. W. "A Note on Ivy Compton-Burnett," *A Review of English Literature*, I (April, 1960), 68-80. A fine analysis, particularly in the relation of wit and style to value judgments.

Johnson, Pamela Hansford. *I. Compton-Burnett*. Bibliographical Series of Supplements to British Book News. London: Longmans, 1951. The first extended critical treatment; although it contains one or two errors, it is written with verve and excitement.

Karl, Frederick Robert. "Ivy Compton-Burnett," *The Contemporary English Novel*. New York: Farrar, Straus & Cudahy, 1962. A reasonable and thorough analysis of the novels.

Kettle, Arnold. *An Introduction to the English Novel*. New York: Harper, 1960. Vol. II, 184-90. An analysis of a passage from *A Family and a Fortune* is used to show that the author just misses the status of a major novelist.

Krieger, Vera P. "An Analytical Study of Children in the Novels of I. Compton-Burnett." Unpublished master's thesis, Bowling Green State University, 1964. A thorough analysis of types of children and their function in relation to plots and themes.

Kunitz, Stanley J., ed. *Twentieth Century Authors*, First Supplement. New York: H. W. Wilson Co., 1955. Valuable for biographical information.

Las Vergnas, Raymond. "Ivy Compton-Burnett," *La Revue de Paris*, LXVIII (September, 1960), 114-21. A general introduction, which seems to draw most of its factual information from Liddell's volume. In French.

Liddell, Robert. *The Novels of Ivy Compton-Burnett*. London: Victor Gollancz, 1955. A devoted and exhaustive treatment of the general qualities of the novels. Although it contains no detailed analyses of individual works, it is the standard critical book.

————. *A Treatise on the Novel.* Appendix III. London: Jonathan Cape, 1947, pp. 146-63. A splendid short treatment by the dean of Compton-Burnett critics. The best short piece on her work.

Mackworth, Cecily. "Les Romans d'Ivy Compton-Burnett," *Critique* (Paris), XIV (May, 1958), 396-404. A good general introduction.

McCabe, Bernard. "Ivy Compton-Burnett, An English Eccentric," *Critique*, III (Winter-Spring, 1960), 47-63. An intelligent general analysis which comes to terms acutely with the general values expressed in the work as a whole.

Newby, P. H. *The Novel 1945-50.* Bibliographical Series of Supplements to British Book News. London: Longmans, 1951. An extremely brief treatment, notable chiefly for its high estimation of Miss Compton-Burnett's chances for permanence of reputation.

Pendry, E. D. *The New Feminism in English Fiction.* Tokyo: Kenkyusha, 1956. A good general introduction, with particular attention to repeated commonplaces and to the sense of anachronism in the works.

Phelps, Gilbert. "The Novel Today," *The Modern Age.* Ed. Boris Ford. Vol. VII, The Pelican Guide to English Literature. Baltimore, Maryland: Penguin Books, 1961, pp. 476-79. A brief, laudatory general introduction.

Prescott, Orville. "Comrades of the Coterie," *In My Opinion.* Indianapolis and New York: Bobbs-Merrill, 1952, pp. 92-109. A hostile treatment that voices the kinds of objections likely to be made by readers who look on the novel simply as a wholesome pastime.

Sackville-West, Edward. "Ladies whose bright Pens . . .," *Inclinations.* London: Secker and Warburg, 1949, pp. 78-103. An urbane and perceptively appreciative treatment of the work.

Sarraute, Nathalie. *The Age of Suspicion.* Tr. Maria Jolas. New York: George Braziller, 1963. The essay "Conversation and Sub-Conversation" explores the possibilities of breaking traditional conventions in the treatment of dialogue, with an appreciation of Miss Compton-Burnett's example of what may be done with this convention.

Snow, Lotus. " 'Good is Bad Condensed': Ivy Compton-Burnett's View of Human Nature," *Western Humanities Review,* X (Summer, 1956), 273-76. A brief and schematized treatment of the types of persons represented in the novels.

Weatherby, W. J. "Tea at Four," *Manchester Guardian,* Air Mail

Edition, LXXXVI (May 17, 1962), 11. An interview with the author in her home.

West, Anthony. "Ivy Compton-Burnett," *Principles and Persuasions.* New York: Harcourt, Brace, 1957. A brilliantly coruscating attack, managed with high intelligence.

Wilson, Angus. "Ivy Compton-Burnett," *The London Magazine,* II (July, 1955), 64-70. A sympathetic, profound analysis of why Miss Compton-Burnett's work just narrowly misses the greatness of Tolstoy, George Eliot, and Dickens.

Index

N. B. The fictional characters listed in this index are largely those whose names appear in the expository passages apart from the treatment of the novel in which they appear. The index does not contain the names of characters whose treatment is confined to the discussion of the novel in which they appear.

Snow, Dr. Lotus, 113, 116, 117, 137
Sophocles, 17
Stace, Andrew *(Brothers and Sisters),* 44, 47, 120
Stace, Sophia *(Brothers and Sisters),* 40, 45-46, 51, 53, 89
Stein, Gertrude, 35
Stevenson, Adlai, 125
Sullivan, Fulbert *(Parents and Children),* 22, 65-66, 93
Sullivan, Nevill *(Parents and Children),* 66-67, 69, 80, 88, 104

Tolstoy, Leo, 112
Turner, Joseph Mallord William, 26

Wake, Julian *(Brothers and Sisters),* 45, 85
Waugh, Evelyn, 49
Way of All Flesh, The by Samuel Butler, 123
Weatherby, W. J., 137
West, Anthony, 112, 128, 138
Wilde, Oscar, 17, 26, 44, 50
Williams, Tennessee, 124
Wilson, Angus, 107, 111-12, 125, 128, 138
Wolsey, Hester *(Mother and Son),* 91-92, 113
Women in Love by D. H. Lawrence, 89
Woolf, Virginia, 23, 36, 38, 112, 119